THE PSYCHOLOGY
OF COURAGE

BY

HERBERT GARDINER LORD

PROFESSOR OF PHILOSOPHY
COLUMBIA UNIVERSITY

BOSTON, MASS.
JOHN W. LUCE & COMPANY
1918

7266
D716

A. 388281

To
M. G. C. L.

TABLE OF CONTENTS

PREFACE

IT may seem to the well-informed reader that the book oversimplifies, and assumes a separateness of the instincts, both of which methods may be thought not in accord with the entangled complexity of the mind of man. The author is not unaware that he is open to this criticism. But he recognizes that all students of mind do and must use both methods. The question of degree is determined by the audience addressed. Instincts, as all mental processes, interpenetrate, often they are but different aspects of the same activity. Understanding comes only through abstraction even for the most knowing.

It also may seem that many things have been omitted which should have been included. The author is only too well aware that he may be open also to this charge. But in a short treatise to serve a special purpose, these unavoidable omissions are inevitable. Perhaps he has been unconscious of certain important aspects of the subject, which maturer thought on a novel problem would have revealed to him.

The book could not have been written but for William McDougall's admirable *Social Psychology*, in which, adopting Shand's concept of sentiments, he has thrown a flood of light on the structure of human mind as it is built by society and which in its turn forms society.

Beyond this, obligations are due to many sources. In the matter of the training of soldiers, assistance was gained from Major (now General) Leroy Eltinge's *Psychology of War*, to which my attention was called by Lieut. Herbert S. Howard, Naval Constructor at Portsmouth Navy Yard. Thanks are especially due to Dr. M. Allen Starr, who has been kind enough to read that part of Chapter XII which deals with so-called shell shock; and also to my colleague, Prof. Munroe Smith, who has read much of the manuscript and given many helpful suggestions.

CHAPTER I

INTRODUCTORY

COURAGE and cowardice have often strange ways with them. At times courage fails us in the most unexpected and unaccountable manner. Again, where we look for cowardice, we see courage stalking heroically across the stage.

For example, a schoolmate was so much of a coward that boys younger in years, smaller in body, and weaker in strength were wont for pastime to thrash him. His name was Howard. The schoolyard at times rang with cries of "Howardy Cowardy." This boy later enlisted in the Northern Army in the Civil War. He became very quickly distinguished for bravery, was promoted from the ranks, was made Aide de Camp, and bore dispatches across fields of death without flinching. Nothing daunted him. How came it about? Another example: two young men, friends, went early in the World War as ambulance drivers to France from an eastern city. In the terrors of their first battle one of them unaccountably turned "yellow." As the saying is, he "crawled under the bed." He was utterly cast down by it, in great despair of himself, dared not hold up his head in face of the world that had honored and respected

1

him as a man of character. What had happened? His comrade who knew him well, a friend indeed, wise in insight, proved his savior. He convinced him that that in him which had failed was not he, that some temporary aberration had seized him. Not many months after there was given this same man the Croix de Guerre for distinguished bravery in battle. How can this be explained? Let us take another instance. A French Lieutenant of Artillery tells of the following case: A soldier at Verdun is in the midst of the severe fire steadily doing his duty, when of a sudden a large shell bursts near him. He throws up his hands and runs away wildly. The lieutenant runs after him, calls him by name. The man seems not to know his officer, who pulls down his hands, leads him back to his place. As the big shells cease to fall just there, the runaway gets busy again with his machine gun. As the lieutenant puts it in his broken English: "When ze large noise stop, ze man forget to be 'fraid and he pomp away at ze Boche wiz his rifle. He laugh and shout 'Pig' at ze Boche." Evidently no coward. Why did he run away then? Examples are many, like that of the "parlor snake," light of weight in character, as everybody thinks, whom girls think good enough to dance with, but not for anything else. Yet this man turns out an officer of ability, of steady, unflinching courage, robust of body and resolute of will, and afraid of nothing. How was it done? Out of a large circle of acquaintance of young college men, all having good promise of success in the affairs of civil life, the greater number have not wanted to go to the horrors and terrors of trench and other warfare in France, and yet they have gone, soberly and unflinchingly, as a matter of course. Why? By that "why" is meant, what is the nature of the mental activity, in this and all the other cases cited, out of which issues what we call courage?

These examples are all taken from war. As many and as striking cases are easily found in civil and domestic life. The nurse who volunteers without a moment's hesitation to attend the loathsome small-pox case, or that of malignant cholera or typhus; the young girl who sacrifices her reputation and social standing to protect her lover from the penalty of wrongdoing; or, on the other hand, the women who, seemingly not of the sort to "quit," yet do forsake unaccountably a post of difficulty and of social danger. And last consider the cases of the men and women who in causes of social reform not only have sacrificed comforts, but beyond that have accepted without a question ill repute and social ostracism; or those others who, in the cause of religious conviction and the establishment of a kingdom of God, which means a just and righteous social order, have suffered not only ill fame in their day, but have faced and achieved martyrdom. In all cases of the kind, is it not possible to discover what it is that takes place in the mental mechanisms of men and women when such things happen, when on the one hand courage is displayed, or on the other, cowardice? And may not the understanding of this matter be of value to those of us who fail, or who would lend a helping hand to others who fail?

It has been suggested that a small book on the Psychology of Courage might be of no little value at the present time. More particularly might it be made valuable to the men and women, whether on battlefield or in trench, in canteen or in hospital, who, by understanding themselves, could thereby be made able better to control in their difficult situations their own emotions, and their own behavior. In this belief this task is here undertaken. Endeavor will be made to disclose to the lay reader what is the nature of courage, how it comes into existence, how it can be strengthened when weak, recovered when lost. Too much is not to be expected from such a treatise, for after all, however much is already known of man's mind and its workings, that much is far too little. This science of the mind is the most difficult of all the sciences. The mind is still largely undiscovered, but what is now known is of immense value and what is of practical importance should be made the possession of as many as possible. To do this for a fragment of man's manifold mental life is the task in hand.

That human nature is, as some hold, a fixed, unchangeable affair, is utterly false. So far from that being true, human nature is from the start by its very inborn constitution to a good degree modifiable. It can be made to develop in various ways into very different forms of mental attitude and behavior. The basic elements may be ineradicable, but they are exceedingly plastic. They are so numerous also, as to be capable of endless varied combination and modification. Thus the varieties of character in individuals, nations and races are very many. The doctrine of inborn fixed national and racial differences, that Germans are by race different from Englishmen, Jews from Gentiles, negroes from whites, like the doctrine of fixed individual differences, is only partially true. German-Americans, Jewish-Americans, Negro-Americans, in the years turn out to be much like English-Americans. They all at last become Americans, very like. This is only possible on the basis of the great modifiability of human nature.

It is on recognition of this fundamental fact that this book is based. Men are not born brave or cowardly as fixed unalterable facts. They may be made either. A man is not born made; he is to be made. Even when made, he can still be remade. How men are made, and how they can, when made after an unfortunate pattern, be remade into another pattern is from one point of view the purpose of this treatise.

CHAPTER II

MECHANISM IN MAN

To understand what courage is and how it comes into being requires some general knowledge of the nature and workings of the mind.

In a certain sense man's mind is a mechanism, a mechanism of extraordinary complexity. "In a certain sense" is a necessary reservation. In using the word mechanism we do not state a fact, but assert an analogy. The mind resembles a machine; it is only in a way one.

The difference which is most important may be brought out in the following way: A moving billiard ball, striking another at rest, sets that other in motion. That is, in its simplest form, mechanical action. Again, a cent dropped into a slot machine causes the machine to put out its bit of chocolate or to indicate one's weight. The cent, a mass of matter like the billiard ball, has struck another mass of matter, a lever, and set it going, and this lever another lever, till the final act has been performed. In both cases there has been what we may call push. The cue has pushed the first billiard ball, and that has pushed the other. The cent has pushed the lever, but the push in the cent is what we call force of gravity. By that word we name not only the movement toward the center of gravity, but its push. When we measure that push we call it weight.

Now the slot machine without that cent dropped in is an inert, non-acting machine. There is no push in it. It needs push from the outside as the billiard ball needs the push of the outside cue, or of another ball. Let us take a more complicated machine, a watch. The wheels and springs may be just what they should be and put together just as they should be, but they are motionless until the spring is wound from the outside by the push of the human hand. Then from the push of the spring the watch acts. Just so to our automobiles, steamships, factories, we add engines which furnish the push to the wheels. In all these mechanisms there are to be noticed two things: first, there is structure of parts into a whole; there is beside some push from the outside added to this structure which causes it to act.

These are illustrations of physical machines, pure and simple. But let us take next a human body, first without, then with, its mind. The body from its very beginning as an ovum, a cell, in the womb, exhibits something of marked difference from the slot machine, the watch, or steamship. It has structure of parts into a whole, as do they. It has also push and of a most extraordinary sort. Its push is not attached to it, added to it from the outside as the winding of the spring to a watch It is within it. The ovum is at once structure and push. From within itself it draws in its food, its fuel, transforms it, becomes two cells instead of one. Each of these from its own inner push becomes two more, then four, eight and so on, indefinitely. But more wonderful still, from within they push into groups, some becoming bone, others muscle, others still lungs, liver, heart, arteries, nerves, eyes, ears, brain. Each is properly placed not from the outside, but from within, each fulfilling also from within its own special function. To be sure, the push in each may be set going, as we shall see, by some stimulus received from another, but the push it exercises when set going is not received from the outside as the cent drives the slot machine or the winding of the spring the watch. The push set going is within itself.

This is the difference between a physical machine and a vital mechanism. No slot machine or watch can act from within itself. It cannot build its own structure, make its own separate parts and organize them together into a systematic whole. Nor can it from within itself operate its own mechanism. Nor can it from within itself produce another of its kind, as the ovum in the womb produces other cells, nor arrange these in a body which can produce other bodies like itself.

There are striking analogies between the two forms of mechanism, but there are more striking differences. Yet through the likenesses we gain understanding of the higher from the lower. It is to be understood throughout our discussion that when the word mechanism is used, it does not mean machine. Between the two notions there is analogy, not identity. In an analogy the difference is as important, if not more important, than the likeness. Not to keep the difference in mind is to expose one's self to fanciful and incorrect thinking. We are likely to think and talk nonsense, without knowing it.

Our concern just now, however, is not so much with the action of the body as with the action of the mind. The description of the structure and self-pushing of the mechanism of the body has been introduced in order to help us understand better the structure and action of the mind. And here we are to use analogy boldly, while being strictly conscious that we are using analogy. We are to talk of the structure of the mind when we cannot lay either eye or hand on this structure. (When we say mind we do not mean brain. We mean consciousness, not nerves.) Because we are aware for fact of acts of mind, and because we are unable to conceive of these acts taking place without structures which act, we come to speak by analogy of mechanisms of the mind, and of those mechanisms as having in themselves the pushes whereby they act. They resemble the living body rather than the made machine. This will become much plainer as we proceed.

Now in the first place, in passing from body to mind, we do find certain mechanisms which can be seen and handled.

For example, the human eye is a species of camera. The light waves strike its sensitive plate, the retina, and chemical action takes place as in the camera.

The eye, however, has what the camera has not. Back of its sensitive plate, or rather wrought into it, are nerve cells, which are charged, we say, with energy; that is, with pushes. These pushes in the eye cells set other pushes going in brain and spinal cord, in muscles, and so muscles contract, limbs move, outside acts are done. But beyond these acts of body and going along with them are mental knowings and feelings.

The camera does not see, the human eye does. Other mechanisms in ear, nose, tongue, give us sound, or odor, or taste. What is a vibration in the ether or in air becomes color or sound. The slot machine does not feel the touch of the cent on the lever. The hand feels. But when we go back of these bodily organs to the knowings and feelings themselves, we cannot, as already has been remarked, find visible and tangible structures. We find acts of mind that are followed by acts of body and other acts of mind. To be sure we have nerve structures in the brain of bewildering complexities which, as the eye is connected with seeing, are certainly connected, in some unknown way, with our various thoughts and emotions. But it is little we know definitely of these. Nevertheless, they are there. They are structures of parts into wholes; that is, mechanisms. The remarkable thing about them is that each of these parts, or nerve cells, is itself not an inert mass, but a push, an energy, potential or active. The wheels, the parts of the watch have not in themselves push. They transmit through themselves pushes received from the outside. The cells, the parts of the nerve mechanism, on the other hand, have in themselves the stored energy to be made active on occasion. They do not transmit a push received. Excited to activity, they push from themselves. Thus it happens that these nerve mechanisms are constructed out of pushes put together. As we think of them from one side, they are to us, as all machines are, things, parts, elements put together. As we look at them from the other side, they are combinations of pushes. A factory is made up of things put together, and pushed by the engine off at one side or below. A nervous system, far more complicated, with a million times more parts than a factory, is not inert things, but millions of pushes, centers of energy, put together. So we can say of it that it is at one and the same time both mechanism and push. It has two aspects, something after the manner of a curve, which, while looked at from one side, is concave, yet, when looked at from the other, is convex. You do not have two separate curves put together, but one curve with its two aspects. So the nerve mechanism has its two aspects. From one point of view it is structure; from the other it is push, energy acting.

But to go back now to the knowings and feelings which we call mind. Beyond and going along with the action of these nerve mechanisms are combinations of various thoughts and feelings. These seem also to have structure. With an arrangement of these ideas and emotions ordered in one way, there follow certain other ideas and emotions, and also certain bodily acts. With another arrangement other acts of mind and body follow. According as is the structure, such is that which follows. In these pure mind-actions we find no tangible or visible organs like eye and ear. We are not aware of any nerve combinations, yet we have actions which imply mechanisms. It is, to be sure, to use analogy boldly. But only so can we understand and express to ourselves and to others something like what happens.

An example will make the matter plain. The ether and air vibrations from a fiercely rushing and barking dog strike the eye and ear of a little child for the first time. The child, in terror, runs away. This is without any previous experience of this or anything like it. Evidently the child is so constructed that when ether and air waves hit eye and ear from just that situation, it will act just in that way in thought, emotion and bodily motion. The whole thing, the structure implied in the act, and the action itself, in perception, emotion, and movement of body, we name instinct. A structure of certain pushes is set going. The light and sound waves do not push into this varied action of mind and body as the cue pushes the billiard ball. These waves put into activity the stored energies, the dormant pushes, so arranged as to behave just that way. The child by inborn structure is set up to act just so.

But now every child born into this world is born

with not only one but with very many of these so-called structures of nervous system and of mind. And during its life it will modify and combine these various inborn structures and so acquire new ones, which, while composed of the inborn elements, will be very different from the elements of which they are compounded, as water, a compound of oxygen and hydrogen, is not like to, but exceedingly different from either.

Courage of various forms will be found to come into existence in the interaction of these original inborn mechanisms, or of those that are later acquired. Thus it will be necessary in another chapter to analyze those innate mechanisms which are found acting in courage.

CHAPTER III

THE INBORN MECHANISMS OF MAN —
OTHERWISE CALLED INSTINCTS

BEFORE naming and describing the various inborn mechanisms that do or may act in courage, certain characteristics of them all should be noted and described.

The first of these is implied in the word chosen to name them, viz.: push. This word, rather than tendency or impulse, has been deliberately chosen because of the peculiar feel that the word excites in the mind when used. Now it will be observed these mechanisms, by reason of their very existence, are busy driving on. Take, for example, the mechanism which appears acting in hunger. When it is in a certain condition, it does not need to await the presence of food to become active. It pushes to find food. The same is true of other appetites like hunger, the mechanisms that urge to drink, to rest, to sleep. The fact of restlessness always denotes the push of mechanisms to their appropriate action. That is what restlessness means and is. Restlessness is removed by finding out what mechanism is pushing and by satisfying it.

The second characteristic to be noted is that when

14

the push of these mechanisms is hindered or interfered with it is increased. Familiar examples are when the horse feels the increased pressure of an up grade, he pulls the more, the dog tugs at his leash the moment he feels its restraint, the child or man meeting a difficulty works the harder. Far different is the case with non-vital mechanical action. The billiard ball on its table pushes toward the earth with a constant, unincreased urgency. The watch with unwound spring is without push; with wound spring has a constant push of a definite strength. Should some bit of sand clog the wheels of it, its spring would not take to pushing the harder. But if you hinder a hungry man going peaceably to his dinner you and he may be amazed at the strength with which you are thrust aside, and that without any conscious action of will.

The third thing that characterizes these mechanisms is the tendency to variation in these pushes. The bullet shot from the rifle strikes and flattens against a stone wall, its push is not only not increased, but its direction also is not changed. But a bee against the window buzzes up and down endlessly. The hungry dog in a cage with food outside does not rush its body against the cage in the direction of the food and stay there. He runs and jumps around in all possible ways, till he either finds a way out or falls exhausted through fatigue. A hungry man pushing toward his food, coming up against a stone wall, climbs over it, goes round it or even knocks it down. He finds a way to his dinner.

The fourth and last characteristic to be considered is that all these mechanisms, so far as they succeed in moving toward their respective ends, are agreeably toned; so far as they fail, they are disagreeably toned. When they get to their ends they stop. We say they are satisfied. We have a twofold sense of satisfaction; that of successful movement toward the end, and that of successful ending of the push. The boy while whittling his stick is an example of the push. The boy having successfully made his kite, or solved his problem, is an example of the second. On the other hand, the hungry boy that cannot find anything to eat, do what he will,' or finding something cannot get at it, is an example of disagreeable toning of his overhindered or defeated mechanism.

These four things will be found true, as we shall see later, of all the mechanisms in man, whether they be inborn or acquired in after life. But just now we are concerned only with inborn mechanisms and not even with all of these. These innate structures are multitudinous, but most of them are irrelevant to our present purpose. Only those that may appear active in courage need be named and described. And even these, as they shall be described, are, as Thorndike has pointed out, complexed out of many varied elements that appear in early infancy, and of which earlier elements no account need here be taken.[1]

The group of mechanisms whose action gives us appetites may be just named in passing. They are such as hunger, thirst, rest, sleep, and, in its lower animal form, sex. What part these play in bringing into existence courage will appear later.

The mechanisms that are now to be named have three parts or aspects in their activity: (1)Each of them knows, is aware of, or perceives a certain kind of object, (2) each exhibits a certain kind of emotion, and (3) each shows a certain kind of bodily action. The list as given by McDougall[2] is as follows:

(a) The fear mechanism or instinct which is set acting by perception of a certain kind of object such as has strangeness, suddenness, fierceness, loud noises, especially when unexpected, or such as darkness, creeping things, etc., giving the emotion of fear or terror and the bodily action of flight.

(b) Disgust mechanism with its characteristic emotion of loathing and its action of ejection from the mouth or withdrawal of the hand or shrinking of body away from.

(c) Curiosity with its emotion of wonder and its motions to examine, approaching and taking apart.

(d) Pugnacity with its emotion of anger and its motion to attack, to injure, or to destroy.

(e) Self-assertion with its emotion of elation and motions of display.

(f) Self-subjection in two forms: first, as humbling one's self to another with its emotion of submission and motions like bowing the head and cringing of body. Second, of following the leader with emotions of submission with pleasure to be led and acts of following joyfully, and elation in obeying

(g) The parental instinct, maternal and paternal, with its tender emotion and acts of protecting, of embracing and fondling.

(*h*) The sex or mating instinct, a higher form of the animal sex *appetite* with its own kind of tender feeling and caressing and other characteristic motions. The brute sex appetite appearing sometimes also in men is without tender emotion.

(*i*) The gregarious instinct with the emotions agreeable in company and disagreeable when alone, and the various motions that take one to the neighborhood of others, to crowds, etc.

(*j*) The instinct of companionship, which is to be distinguished from the gregarious instinct since it is more particular, seeking individual comrades. It pushes to contact by touch, while gregariousness finds content in contact by sight of the crowd. Its emotion is tender, but of a quality different from that of either parental or sex affection. It is the basis of friendship, comradeship. The merely gregarious man pure and simple haunts crowds, lives in cities, cannot abide the country, but shuns companionships, avoids friendships. The companionship man cannot live without comrades and friends, but may get along well without crowds, even may avoid them. He may feel never more alone than in a crowd.

(*k*) The acquisitive instinct, with its emotion of gloating over, and its motor action of seizing and holding.

(*l*) The instinct of rationality, with its intellectual emotions and its motions of body expressive of thought. By rationality is meant not only or not so much logical reasoning as rational insight.[3]

These are all called specific tendencies, or instincts, because in each case a certain particular kind of object sets each going with its certain kind of emotions and its certain kind of bodily action. For example, a dangerous kind of object sets off the flight instinct, with its fear emotion and its bodily acts of escape; an angering object sets going the instinct of pugnacity with its emotion of rage, and its bodily acts to attack, injure, or kill; the child sets going the parental instinct, with its emotion of love and motions of protection and caressing. In each there is something particular that awakes particular feelings and movements.

Beside these more special and definite, there are several more general mechanisms that appear in pushes to certain acts of mind or body. The first to be mentioned is suggestion, whereby are received ideas thrust into the mind by others, from which issue acts of body according to these ideas. This appears in its most complete form in hypnotism. But men quite generally are prone to take suggestions. So we get not only most of our beliefs, scientific and religious, but thousands of traditional ways of thinking about the weather, the Constitution of our country, and the sanctity or otherwise of the Republican or Democratic party. And we perform without conscious willing, and even without being aware of it, innumerable acts, the idea of which is suggested to us by others. All men are, as a rule, susceptible to suggestion; many are very highly so.

The second general mechanism is sympathy, by which we catch, as by contagion, modes of feeling from others. We rejoice with those that rejoice, mourn with those that mourn, get excited when others are, and the like, without much, if any, intellectual activity, seemingly sometimes the less the more excitement. By reason of this we get in a panic of fear among the fearing without an idea of why. This mechanism seems closely connected with, perhaps is indeed a form of the action of, the gregarious instinct.

The third general mechanism is that which pushes to imitation. By this we acquire, largely without conscious copying, our so-called native tongue, characteristic national, or racial, or class manners, as well as accept as a matter of course our fashions of dress and social behaviors. Through the action of this also come in part our panics, by which we find ourselves running away from the enemy without rhyme or reason with others headed in the same direction. By this also we may even find ourselves with as little rhyme or reason running forward against the foe.

The last general mechanism needing to be named as having to do with courage is temperament The description of this is very difficult. But what is meant by the word is quite well known. Men by temperament are optimistic or pessimistic, are sanguine and hopeful, or are shrinking and despairing, are adventurous, aggressive and progressive, or averse to change and conservative. Temperament will play, as it will be seen, no small part in the structures that act in courage.

These mechanisms are properly named general because, as will be seen, neither the objects that set them going, nor the activities that result, are so specific as in the former class For example, any one of all the inborn or acquired mechanisms can be set going by suggestion. So also the emotions characteristic of each can be aroused in sympathy, and bodily acts peculiar to each can be called into existence by imitation. As for temperament, it will modify, or determine to a great degree, the manner of action of all instinctive and acquired or specific and general tendencies.

The list as here given is very far from complete. But enough has been named to furnish the material needed for the purposes of this study.

There are two characteristics of all these mechanisms, both the special and the general, that must now be described. They both, in accordance with our accepted analogy, can also be named mechanisms, in that they show that we are set up in such a manner as to cause us to act in certain ways. The first is that of habit formation. From earliest life, doubtless before as well as after birth, ways of acting tend to become fixed. Prior to this and going along with it is, of course, the tendency to variety of activity of each of these mechanisms. Because of this tendency to fix, and the other tendency to vary forms of acting, learning is possible. Without the first, nothing done could be retained. Without the second, nothing new could be taught and learned. All teaching and all learning involves the existence of a mechanism that can retain and can vary. What on the one hand teaching acts upon, what on the other learns, are these mechanisms. Because they

are, and because they are what they are, at once
for fixation and for flexibility, education is possible.

The other characteristic tendency is the push of
these various mechanisms to unite, to combine into
systems. The separate mechanisms not only combine in something of a mechanical way, as when the
dog dodges the whip while rushing for the bone, or
when the curious boy goes timidly and hesitatingly
into the dark corner, but, as will be shown later, they
may complex themselves into elaborate systems.

The original or inborn difference between one man
and another is caused by the difference in the relative
strength and flexibility of these native mechanisms.
It may be presumed that he is a rare man who is
born with some one or more of them left out, as
he is a rare man who is born without eyes.

Although they are included in the foregoing statement, it may be wise to single out for special mention
the general tendency or mechanism apparent in
habit formation, and the tendency to the uniting and
complexing of the inborn special instincts into systems, which is a special kind of habit formation.
Men vary greatly by native structure both in the
ease in which habits are formed and persist, and yet
retain flexibility, and also in the capacity to combine the special and general mechanisms into complex systems. Some can form relatively few habits
and those only into unmodifiable combinations.
Some retain flexibility, even into an advanced age,
while others early become hardened into what are
called fossils and after that remain quite changeless.

Others are capable of forming vast and elaborate systems of mechanisms, and systems of systems, and seem scarcely ever unable to modify and remodel old combinations, to meet new and changing situations. While it may be impossible to teach an old dog a new trick, it is sometimes possible for an aged man to appropriate new ideas, change his creed and vote with another party.

It will be observed that in this list there has not appeared any mention of an inborn structure or mechanism that could be named courage. In fact, courage is not in itself an instinct. It comes into being in and through the action of structures that are inborn or acquired. It is the name for the action of these structures or mechanisms under certain conditions.

We are now in a position to describe how courage in its simpler forms comes into existence and just what is its nature. And it may be more profitable to describe these simpler forms before going on to describe the complex acquired mechanisms that are built up out of these original inborn mechanisms and in the action of which complex acquired mechanisms the higher and nobler forms of courage arise. This will be well, though much that is to be said of these simpler forms of courage will be true also of the more complex and higher forms.

CHAPTER IV

The Nature of Courage

As was remarked in the last chapter, the inborn structures in man push spontaneously into their own characteristic activities. They may not wait on outside pushes as do mechanical contrivances. They may, when in a certain condition, take to pushing of themselves. Even when set going by some outside stimulation, it is they that then act from a push within. Now all these mechanisms may be hindered in their actions by obstructions of various kinds. Sometimes the obstruction comes from conditions altogether outside, at other times the activity of one mechanism can interfere with, even stop, the activity of another. It is just in this state of affairs that what we call courage appears. In all forms of it, it is the overcoming or bearing up against resistances to the activity of certain mechanisms, inborn or acquired.

These particular pushes against resistances to which are given the name courage may be grouped in three classes.

There is first the push to overcome outside difficulties, as when we say, "You are a brave man to attack such a job as that," or "You have more courage than I have to face such difficulties." A man might be unwilling to undertake to reorganize a bankrupt railway system, or to take command of a great army, or even to marry a woman with numerous children whom he might very deeply love. And in each case not because the instinct of fear is set going, but simply because the task is felt to be beyond his abilities, or involves expenditures of thought and effort, of time and energy, beyond what he is willing or in the circumstances is able to give. To surmount such obstacles is not courage properly so called, nor what is generally meant by that word. It may perhaps in most cases be called self-reliance. It arises pre-eminently from that inborn mechanism called self-assertion, which pushes to override and delights in surmounting difficulties, and seeks its satisfaction just in feeling one's self masterful. Its opposite is not cowardice, but rather discouragement.

Other instincts may have part in this, as, for example, the "wanderlust," which, after all, may be but a variant form of the powerful push of self-assertion, combined with the hunting instinct, which in turn, may at first have been a varied form of the hunger push. Men urged by this instinct are adventurous, restless souls, pushed on as hunters, pioneers, not only into untravelled parts of earth, but unexplored realms of thought and feeling. The instinct of fear may be, and doubtless often is, complicated with this form of courage, but it need not necessarily be so.

Another form of courage arises when the inborn

or acquired structures are thwarted by resistances either from outside circumstances or inner interfering activities. Take, for example, the simple case when one must go hungry for lack of food. In such case one man whines, another bears his suffering without a murmur. Again, another man is born a cripple and throughout life is greatly handicapped and yet lives valiantly. Or another, a Charles Lamb, cannot marry because of an afflicted sister for whom he must care, and utters no protest. The examples are numerous of this kind of courage. Life is full of such brave men, and more often of such brave women, who do their job and give no sign of asking any approval or compassion. Here again no activity of the instinct of fear may be found. Sometimes, perhaps oftener than is apparent, some form or degree of fear may enter in, but it need not be present at all and often is not. This form of courage is properly fortitude. It may be doubted if it ever exists on the lower level of one instinct overriding another instinct. It requires a developed mind for its existence.

We come now to the class of courages which are properly so called and which we almost always mean by that word. In this class what obstructs is the action of the instinct of fear. The action of other instincts pushing to their satisfactions is checked by the action of this instinct. The curious boy, no matter how desperately curious to know what is in that dark hole, never will dare explore it. Curiosity, though strong, is stopped absolutely from pushing out into overt activity, but it still goes on pushing in spite of fear and disturbs him endlessly. If he can get some braver boy to explore with him, his restlessness subsides, his ceaseless push of curiosity gains its satisfaction and stops. There is then the comfort of rest. The brave boy in this particular case may be simply the boy whose instinct of curiosity is more vigorous in its action than his instinct of fear. Or it may be that his instinct of self-assertion combines with his instinct of curiosity and overwhelms so easily the activity of the instinct of fear that in his case the obstruction of fear is reduced to a minimum.

In all cases falling in this class of courages, the instinct of fear is overridden by some other instinct acting more vigorously. Conversely, cowardice is the overriding of the activity of other instincts by the more vigorous activity of fear. According to the relative native strength of this instinct of fear in regard to other instincts, men are born courageous or cowardly.

Before going on, it should be thoroughly understood that by the word fear is always meant the particular mechanism that is characterized by the inner emotion of fear and the outer bodily movements of flight, together often with many other forms of physical expression, such as crouching, trembling, creeping of hair, sweating, turning pale, chills, at first the slowing, then the quickening of heart-beat and breathing, and many less apparent changes in the normal action of bodily organs.

By the action of this mechanism man, like other animals, is made averse to meeting dangerous situations. But fear is but one of many aversions, and should not be confounded with them. As was stated in a former chapter, mechanisms checked or balked when pushing on to their proper satisfactions are toned disagreeably. Aversion is a name for that fact. In our usual way of using our language very loosely, we are wont to call all these aversions fears. We say we are afraid of going hungry, losing sleep, being cold. We call all our aversions to petty as well as to greater discomforts fears. But in none of them may there appear any of the characteristics of emotion and bodily reaction which belong to fear proper. Fear, however, may be complicated with them, that is the fear mechanism may be set acting by and through the checking of other mechanisms.

Although by general consent, fear oftener than not is that which has to be overcome, in courage, it is not the only instinct that for fact is to be resisted. One of the strongest of these is disgust. It may or may not be complicated with fear. A young friend physically strong and athletic, going to France and into trench warfare, remarked that what repelled him even more than the danger was the loathing for the dirt and vermin. It was easier for him to override instinctive fear than disgust.

But it is especially disgust in the form of horror, which certainly is not fear proper and unmixed, that must be overcome. This drives a man away from sights of wounds, blood, lacerations, pains, agonies.

We have in this a mingling of disgust with its emotions of loathing of sympathetic pain, in which pity is largely lacking, and which creates an impulse sometimes violent to withdraw. It is well nigh impossible for some men to withstand this push, harder than to face proper situations of fear. There are men of intense imagination and sympathy who faint in bayoneting sandbags. These men have a horror of killing even an enemy who is not to be feared. In fierce anger of battle it can be swamped, as can fear, but it is not fear only that makes some men reluctant to enter the trenches and slow to face battle horrors.

There is another instinct, which, unsatisfied and combining with fear, makes courage a necessity. It is the instinct of companionship. With many it is very strong. Revolt against leaving home and intimate comrades and going off alone, rather than fear, holds such men back from going across far seas to distant France. This instinct is other than gregariousness, for there will be the herd of many men about them, but as they look out upon it, not comrades, at least not as yet, perhaps never. The confession of such reluctance has been made by young men who have gone, nevertheless, and as volunteers. This required courage, but it was not fear that had to be overcome. The action of this instinct at its extreme was in the bitter cry of the dying boy to his father, "Must I go alone?"

A significant recognition of the reality of the working of this instinct of companionship to increase

courage in war is found in the practice of Prince
Frederick Charles in the War of 1866. "He permitted
friends and relatives to be placed in the same squad
though of different heights. A company formed in
this way would not look so well on parade, but it
could be expected to give a better account of itself
in battle.[4]"

But coming back to courage and cowardice proper,
as the overcoming of fear or the being overcome by
it, we are in a position now to ask what we mean by
the fearless man. Strictly speaking, there perhaps
never existed any such man, and if he existed he
could not be a brave man. He would be a man without the instinct of fear in him, a defective, like the
man born without eyes. He could no more take
credit to himself for not being afraid than could the
blind man for not seeing obscene sights. Such a fearless man would be a monstrosity. When we speak
of the brave man who is fearless, we mean the man
who, though afraid, overcomes his fear. Courage
would, then, have to be measured not only in terms
of the strength of instinct overcoming fear, but in
terms of the strength of the fear instinct that is
overcome. Terribly afraid, but going ahead nevertheless, means more courage than somewhat afraid
of the dangers involved and violent anger overwhelming fear. To be well aware of the danger, and
shaking with terror and yet going on all the same,
or all the more — that, indeed, is courage. That is
what we mean by the fearless man. The Grand
Marshal Vendome of France, a little man on his big

white horse in the very midst of the firing (such was the custom of commanders in his day), noticing his trembling body, says, "Art afraid, little body? If thou knewest where I am going to take thee, thou wouldst be afraid indeed." When a man on going into battle boasts he is not afraid, if he is not a mental defective, he is lying. All normal men are afraid. That is why they can be brave. He who is not afraid cannot be brave. He who is brave must of necessity be afraid. The measure of his courage is in the violence of his fear successfully overcome.

It should be remarked that the three different modes of behavior called courage may, and often do, combine. The soldier in the trenches may find, in the extraordinary difficulties of that life, a situation calling out all his abilities to master them and face them courageously as difficulties. Also the hungers, deprivations, exposures to cold and other inclemencies of weather, and to pains of disease may arouse his courage as fortitude to superior activity. And still again he may face the actual terrors of battle and imminent danger of death without quailing. Courage in all its forms may be fused into unity in his mental life and bodily action in so complex a situation.

CHAPTER V

THE SIMPLER AND LOWER FORMS OF COURAGE FROM THE POINT OF VIEW OF THE INBORN MECHANISMS

THOUGH it may be certain that in adult life rarely, if ever, does any single instinct act altogether alone, yet it will be of present advantage to proceed as though instincts do so act. Getting clearness by such arbitrary simplification, we shall afterward win clearness of view in understanding the actual complexes that would otherwise appear to us confused messes. Thus in this chapter no attempt will be made to draw a line between the simpler and more complex, the higher and lower forms of courage. There exists in fact no such clear division between them.

It will be apparent to the most superficial consideration that the one instinct most often, if not always, acting in courage as commonly understood is pugnacity. Other inborn mechanisms when thwarted in their push to satisfaction, are apt to set going this mechanism of fighting with its emotion of anger. It may be questioned if ever pugnacity acts without the balking of another instinct.

This matter of courage on the level of instinct can

be admirably illustrated from the animal world. We speak of the lion as king of beasts and say "brave as a lion," "Richard, the Lion-hearted." But the lion is in one situation a coward as he is brave in another. This is shown in a recent article in the *Atlantic Monthly* written by one who has had wide opportunity to observe. The lion driven by the push of hunger is easily made angry. The more hunger he feels, the more furious he becomes. Then it is anger added to his hunger that drives him on viciously. So, also, if, when feeding and satisfying his hunger, he is interrupted in the process, he becomes furious and charges his interrupters, no matter what or how many they are. But when his hunger is satisfied and its urgency at rest, he will run away as any coward or timid antelope. If, however, in his flight, *i.e.*, in his fear activity, he is balked, his anger is aroused, his mechanism of anger is set going and as that in him is a very strong mechanism, he is driven violently forward in attack against great odds. But in this he differs in no respect from very timid small animals, whose safety depends oftener on the strength of their fear mechanism, rather than on any other instinct. The little rat cornered by to him the monster man will attack viciously. The mother hen with her brood about her charges valiantly the same monster man who seems to endanger her offspring. Here the maternal protective instinct balked by the enemy sets off anger, the fighting instinct, and though equipped with a very ineffective weapon, her bill, she none the less, with a lion heart, charges home. In the same way the timid woman becomes a vicious fighter when the safety of her babe is at stake.

The like appears in the activity of the sex mechanism, one of the strongest in man. With or even without arousing the fighting instinct, it may override the fear instinct utterly. When its push for long has not received its accustomed satisfaction, when suddenly and unexpectedly in its then hypersensitive condition it is aroused to action, it drives on in utter blindness to all perils. Here exists, seemingly, the very condition of the lion heart of the half-famished lion. It is on the same psychological level. From this point of view we can understand the act of a white soldier from the North attacking an eleven-year-old girl near a southern camp. First in aroused fighting instinct he attacks and routs her boy companion who obstructs his passion. When some months afterwards he is being led to the scaffold, he remarks that he is getting what he deserves. If wildly excited in battle, his instinct of anger had thrust him as ruthlessly through perils to fearless deeds, he would have received the medal for distinguished service. He then, too, would have got what he deserved. Alike in the utter subjugation of fear there is difference in what tramples fear under foot. If we may not call the first cowardice, we do call it brute. We may perhaps honor in excess the second in calling it courage, though it certainly is such on a lower instinctive brute level. The cruder, more primitive type of Southern negro, though faced with all the horrors of burning at the stake, in his attack on the white woman "carries on" over all terrors, blinded to them all. It is a case of the lion heart of the hungry brute again. Why not brave? We never call it so.

In milder forms this instinct, as in courting, pushes the lover to visit his lady-love when it is to his great disadvantage. I recall the following telegram to a lady from a man kept by her family over long from looking on her beloved face: "I'll see you in spite of hell this morning." What was hell to a hungry lover in that excited state?

If courage, then, be the overcoming of fear, it is clear that it makes a vast difference as to what are the mechanisms inborn or acquired by which fear is subdued.

There is one inborn mechanism that more than any other when thwarted arouses the fighting instinct and which, when pugnacity is aroused, more than any other leads to conflict and the subjugation of fear. This is the instinct of self-assertion. This mechanism is at one with the very essence of life, which pushes to its own persistence in being and to its expansion. To check either is to tend to restrict, to destroy life. This mechanism is at the root of all our egotism, vanity, pride, adventuresomeness, our selfishness, our will to power, our love of mastery. In our poultry yard it sets cocks at each other; in the herd it hurls bulls at each other, in our drawing-rooms it makes our cultured ladies "cats," in business our church pillars become cut-throat competitors, in international relations, more than aught else, it brings on the horrors of ruthless warfare between the most civilized and Christian nations. It is, however, as well at the root of our forcefulness, enterprise, proper pride and self-respect; from it issue in great part our heroisms and sanctities, our lofty aspirations and our high achievements in whatever field of human endeavor.

But just now the one aspect of this self-assertion, with which we are here concerned, is its place in the creation of courage. It seems more intimately than any other instinct to be identified with the very core of one's self. To have it overridden is like, if it is not in very fact, losing one's soul. What indeed will not a man give to save his soul? So there is nothing in which a man is more sensitive, by checking which he is more easily made angry, nothing that in man may with the aroused fighting instinct more violently trample fierce fears underfeet. Thus courage is aroused by making one conscious that his self-importance, his vanity even, too often called honor, is injured or violated.

Further and more complete discussion of this element in overcoming fear will be postponed to the exposition of the higher levels of courage.

In passing, something may be said concerning the curious forms of sham courage of the bully and the braggart. Both are self-asserters of a very pronounced type. The bully, whose instinct of fear is relatively very strong, asserts himself in situations in which his fear mechanism is not greatly aroused.

He lords it over little boys in the playground. He asserts himself where others are unable or unwilling to strike back. Social bullies are of both sexes. This is sufficient to make clear why bullies are called and are cowards.

In like manner the braggart being strongly endowed with the fear mechanism and strong in self-assertion, brags where his fear is not aroused, and is immediately silent when and where it is.

Foolhardiness, while a genuine courage, a courage based on self-assertion and overriding fear easily, is courage without intelligence gained by experience. It is often closely allied to the courage of the braggart, in that both are in this case based on vanity. The schoolboy, and boys of even an advanced age, " will not be stumped." They risk life, even lose it, rather than be thought or think themselves cowards. Rev. Frederick W. Robertson, a man of noblest character and one of the very greatest of English preachers, tells us that he at one time delivered a sermon which he knew was unwise, and would do no good but only mischief, simply because he happened to think he was afraid to preach it. Kingdon Clifford, a foremost scientist of England in the last century, on a dare hung by his toes from a cross on a church spire On a dare a college friend, of really high character, read in class from an English translation a long paragraph of a Latin author — a dishonorable act for which he has never been able to forgive himself. The cases of soldiers, even officers, giving up lives invaluable to their country, in this

kind of subjugation of fear are numerous. To this
kind of overriding fear we refuse the name of
courage proper.

The instinct of acquisition, which works to get and
keep, is naturally averse to loss. As so averse, it
overrides not only difficulties that interfere with
getting, but interferences that would take away.
Such resistance is not courage in the sense of overcoming fear proper. But when in addition to the
aversion to loss the mechanism of fear is excited,
and checked acquisition arouses also the mechanism
of pugnacity, then we have courage truly so called.
Fear, originating in the first instance in the thwart-
ing of the active mechanism of acquisition, is overridden by the anger which is also aroused.

The part played in building courage by the general
mechanisms described in a previous chapter will be
made plain when the higher levels are considered.

There are certain other ways contributory to the
overcoming of fear that should not be neglected.
The wild beast is called wild, because, through the
action of its mechanism of fear, it runs away from
the strange, and therefore to it dangerous, man or
situation. It may come, through repetition and
familiarity, to a state in which the mechanism will
not be made active. So squirrels, timid creatures by
nature, come to eat out of one's hand when their
instinct of fear is not set going, and the man has
become familiar to them. So birds will alight on the
scarecrow, and wrens build their nests over one's
head on the veranda. We are not wont to speak of

the courage of our domesticated wild animals, because they have ceased to be afraid of us. Yet there appears in them the working of a psychological law which has wide bearing on the building of certain forms of courage.

We have a proverb, "Familiarity breeds contempt." It indicates but one aspect of a much broader principle. When we *get used to* the ticking of the clock we cease to hear it. We can get used to, come not to hear, the racket of a boiler factory, in the trenches well nigh to the roar of constant canonading; can get used to, not mind, dangerous situations, that is, though they be there in reality, not pay attention to them. When we do attend we become at once afraid. Veterans arrive by repetition of experience at this state of familiarity that breeds in a large degree indifference, inattention to the dangerous.

Though indifference to dangerous situations may be a very valuable element in the courage of a veteran, it has its own defects. It tends to carelessness, *i.e.*, not with care paying attention to dangers that are really there. Many a veteran has paid the penalty of just being a veteran. It is not the mark of bravery carelessly to ignore dangers. That kind of a fearless man, fearless by acquired mechanism of that sort, is not a desirable soldier. A good soldier is expected always to have his fear mechanism in excellent working order. Indeed, if he is not constantly afraid, he is no good. All too soon he is in a hospital or cemetery, and the foe has the field.

We have last to consider for a little a manner in which fear is weakened and overcome, while courage properly so called is not produced. And yet in warfare the matter is of great importance. For example, the wild beast, which means the beast whose instinct of fear works actively in what to it is danger, may be tamed by hunger. This means that the push of its hunger may be so vigorous as to drive it to food in spite of perils. The fear push is simply swamped by the hunger push. Men may be driven, through lack of food, into a certain degree of bravery. Something of this appeared according to report, when, previous to the recent Austrian drive into Italy, her hungry soldiers were told that they could get plenty to eat in Lombardy. But it was noticed there was small pushing power in those hungry Austrian soldiers. The accuracy of this report may well be doubted. But for purposes of illustration it is useful, if not altogether true. Commanders of armies do not starve their soldiers to make them brave. Though some use may be made in its first stages of the urgency of hunger which has come unsought, yet the lack of nourishment to the whole system, which is involved in hunger, may reduce the urgency of all mechanisms active in courage, while increasing the push of the fear mechanism. It is a matter of observation that a weakened organism is more susceptible to fear than a vigorous one. Human mechanisms all depend on food and without it they weaken and may stop. On this account the courage of an army must be kept up by good feeding. The mechanism of hunger must be satisfied, if there is to be vigorous action of the mechanisms of fighting, and all other mechanisms which may be called in to support and re-enforce these. So it may happen that the German army, to a certain extent, may be tamed, may have the fight taken out of it, by a blockade of foodstuffs. And that it shall not have the fight taken out of it in that way, the civilian population of Germany goes meagerly fed that the army may be brave. And we in America go without certain foods that not only the allied peoples be fed, but that their courage and the courage of their armies be maintained. In this way it can be seen that courage is to a degree a matter of the Quartermaster Department. It undertakes to protect the soldier from getting tamed, that is from a reduction to a low level of vigor of the fighting mechanisms. This is one way, though not by any means the only or most effective way, in which the morale, as we call it, of an army can be lowered. But given this fundamental physical necessity for food well supplied, courage becomes a matter of mind or spirit, first of instinctive endowment; later, of acquired disposition. Cowards, as well as brave men, may be well fed. Starving men are not so likely to be brave.

It was stated above that the instinct, which is most likely to overcome fear on the lower level of courage, is pugnacity. In battle, arousing the fighting spirit means getting soldiers fighting, often crazy mad. It is on the level of, in fact is, brute courage.

This is generally known as physical courage. It is, in fact, courage on the instinctive level, above which brutes never rise. Sometimes alcoholic drinks are used as a means to this end. It is now demonstrated that alcohol for the time weakens, even may break down, higher connections of the brain, and so bring about action on an approximate instinctive level. It is known that many, perhaps most men, are more easily angered under the influence of liquor. Their courage, as mere angry fighting urgency, is more reckless in such a condition. But also it is less reliable. It tends to the transientness characteristic of all intense emotional states. Mind fatigues rapidly under these conditions, and reaction from them is apt to set in when least expected, and at dangerous crises. Fear is always crouching and ready to spring into violent action in a state of nerves that ensues on exhaustion, for fear is among the very strongest of all inborn mechanisms. It is, biologically considered, one of the earliest mechanisms to appear, and life for long ages has been able to survive through its effective working. Even men, creatures of a late day, tend to revert to its action all too easily. And its uncontrolled working is what cowardice in fact most often is. This long life history and great inborn strength of this instinct explains its sudden, startling, extremely unwelcome appearance. In certain conditions of nervous tention, or unwariness of attention, or strangeness of outside conditions, it overwhelms one without warning, and to one's utter shame and undoing. To understand this is a great help in recovering ones' self-respect, and so one's courage. Also, it reveals to us the certainty that there is no mastery of fear worth a thought on the instinctive level. No one can command at will anger, or any other instinct, to forestall fear's sudden onrush, or, when it is under its violent way, can switch to other mechanisms the currents of instinctive action. The only method possible is the building up of acquired structures, which the dangerous situations shall awake to action, instead of instinctive fear. The strength and massiveness of these structures under the guidance of intelligence; that is, of ideas, or reason, can override instinctive fear. Nothing else can do this effectively and enduringly. So we turn in the following chapters to the study of the nature and methods of constructing these acquired mechanisms which bring into existence higher forms of courage.

CHAPTER VI

Acquired Complex Mechanisms Working in Higher Forms of Courage

In the preceding chapter notice was called to the fact that repetition made one used to, indifferent to, inattentive to something that at first excited fear. This is technically called "negative adaptation." It may have occurred to one that the inborn mechanisms set up by inheritance to act in a certain way, when set going, must have become modified in structure in order to act so differently, or to cease to act at all when there is present the same stimulus or object. This change in structure is called acquired to distinguish it from what is native. It is acquired mechanism in its simplest form. No new structure is built. Only some modification of inborn structure is effected. That is all. Modification of structure of this form goes on throughout life. By it we become used to comforts as well as discomforts. We accept far too easily, as matters of course, the loving ministrations of mother and wife, even perhaps without noticing that they are given. If they stop, we receive the same sort of shock that comes to us when the clock stops.

But again in the last chapter another sort of

modified inborn structure appeared. The separate
native mechanisms were seen to act together in
combination, each modifying the activity of each.
For example, the fear of the mother whose babe is
attacked becomes fused with her anger. The excitement of her fear is a powerful stimulant to her
pugnacity. She fights more fiercely as her inborn
love for her babe and her fear for its safety are
both aroused. Here are fused three mechanisms.
No wholly new mechanism is in.roduced. It is the
working together of several separate mechanisms
which in other situations might be made active
separately. When now we have built together into
a permanent unified structure several of these
original inborn mechanisms, we get acquired mechanisms that are not simply modifications of single
mechanisms nor temporary combinations. They are
lasting organizations into complexes, with characteristic ways of acting peculiar to themselves. They
have been named sentiments by Shand, Stout, and
McDougall,[5] whose work in this field of inquiry
seems in the main to be increasingly accepted by
psychologists, and whose results are frankly adopted
in this treatise.

Illustrations will make plain what is meant. Take
the maternal instinct awakened in the mother by
the birth of her child. The child in danger, the
mother's fear is aroused. The child's beauty denied,
or a hint given of defects in her child, the mother's
anger is set going. The babe is seen to be the center
from which different mechanisms in the mother are

made active. As the child develops, manifesting the possession of all manner of admirable qualities, the mother's idea, conception, of her child develops into an increasingly rich complexity, and her child becomes the center from which any number of emotions may be set going in the mother. Let her son achieve distinction in school, college, in business, in battle, there will awake in her an exceedingly rich and multifarious blend of emotions. All emotions, but hate will be in the complex. This is called the sentiment of love. It is a mechanism of vast and intricate inter-relations ready to spring into manifold forms of activity on the instant that occurs the sight or thought of that son in different situations of achievement or failure, of honor or shame.

Perhaps an even better illustration is the growth of a sentiment in the child for the mother, since in the undeveloped intelligence of the babe, at first no mechanisms but the primitive ones of hunger and bodily comfort are acting. And there is no evidence of a filial instinct. The mother to its infant eyes, as first seen, is nothing but a spot of moving color. As the days go by, that moving color not only grows more distinct and complex, it gets to the growing boy new meanings. That once mere spot of color out there comes to be a person who feeds him, fondles him, comforts him in pain, plays with him, clothes him, supplies him with numberless desirable things. On this basis of his instinct of companionship, the mother excites in him joys, love, admiration, respect, strange and delightful emotional experiences.

He, to be sure, does not analyze, is not capable of analyzing his varied experiences which have their source in his mother. But as the idea of his mother has developed in him into an exceedingly complex thing, so his emotional responses have developed. Is her life in danger, he is in terror. Is she insulted, he is in a rage. When she is honored, her beauty admired, her wit applauded, her character praised, he swells with pride and rejoices. Beneath his hat he carries always this highly complex mechanism. For days or months it may not be acting. But if in the midst of his affairs in distant lands a letter from her arrives, or if only the thought of her floats into his mind, the mechanism of his sentiment works, and perhaps violently in joy or sorrow, according as is the thought of her, as in health or sickness, in prosperity or disaster, awakened by letter or in imagination.

It is only necessary to mention the case of casual meeting of one man by another. Each at first is only a man to each. As meetings multiply, acquaintance continues, the idea each has of each will develop and there may grow up in each the complex mechanism of a sentiment of friendship, or perhaps of enmity. In the former case what we call love, the tender emotion will be the central inborn mechanism or instinct characterizing the sentiment. In the latter case pugnacity, push to injure or even to destroy, will be the characteristic emotional and motor impulse of the sentiment we call hate. To meet your enemy on the street is to be impelled to punch him, or at least to swear under your breath. Your face is pulled into rigidity. Your fists clench while you force out a greeting as hollow as it is angering. Should such men separate and not meet for years, they might come to be unaware of what each is to each. Yet the mention of the name of one to the other would awaken the long-dormant sentiment into even violent activity. Long separation without correspondence or recall in memory, of course, may weaken a sentiment of friendship, may even cause it to disappear. Yet it is seldom that any well-built sentiment altogether disappears.

It will be observed that these mechanisms, like the instincts out of which they are organized, are in consciousness only when they are awakened into action. They are abiding structures below conscious life with their stored pushes or energies, most of them held in check by other structures which are at any given time acting, or by systems of structures that permit the instinctive elements, of which they are composed, to act only when the systems as a whole act. This is the vast realm of the unconscious of which so much is said at the present time. Sentiments, then, in the technical sense, are neither conscious ideas or feelings, but they are structures, because of which certain thoughts and feelings will arise when the structures are made active.

These complexes, acquired by building together inborn emotional mechanisms around the ideas of objects, are very numerous. We are inhabited by thousands of them, perhaps oftener than not quite

unknown to us, till some sudden presentation of an
object awakes us with a shock to the fact that such
a sentiment is ours. We have them for persons we
think we are totally indifferent to, for places and
communities in which we fancy ourselves altogether
without any interest. A line in a newspaper to the
credit or discredit of a man to whom we fancy ourselves indifferent, awakens our pleasure or regret.
A word against what we call our "God forsaken
town" makes us angry. A college mate whom we
never could like, met in after years in a distant city,
is greeted with pleasure. A German-American friend,
who imagined himself thoroughly American, on the
outbreak of the war in 1914, confessed that he was
"appalled to discover how much of a German" he
was. Another man, fancying that he had lost all
acceptance of Christianity, was astonished to find,
on the outbreak of this war with its violation of all
Christian ideals, how dear were to him the principles
of Christ.

Enough has been said, it may be presumed, to
make plain the reality of these multitudinous mechanisms called sentiments built up in us out of
combinations of inborn instincts. It remains now
to see how out of certain of these acquired complex
mechanisms are developed the more complex higher
forms of courage.

These acquired complex mechanisms, which have
been named sentiments, work precisely as do the
original inborn instincts. They are not ordered,
organized *things* into machines. They are organized

pushes, and like hunger, fear, anger, they push to their satisfactions when awakened with a violence proportioned, on the one hand, to their intrinsic strength, on the other, to the vigor of the stimulus that sets them acting. We long for converse with our friends, not that there is anything particular to be said, but the emotional dispositions, our sentiments toward them, need active satisfaction. If we are far from them, we are impatient for letters. We take a look at the picture of the true love, handily in our pocket, to arouse the better the pushing love sentiment that gains so some inadequate, though real, satisfaction in its proper activity. These structures of sentiments may rush as fiercely into action as the lion toward his prey. For example, a man learning that his mother, or even a friend, is in a burning building, may madly dash in to the rescue. Fear is overridden as easily as it is by the man crazed with anger. We are apt not to think so much of the courage of the man thus acting as of the crazed state of his mind. Without his strong abiding sentiment of love he could not be crazed, as without the strongly aroused instinct of anger another man could not go crazy mad.

From this point of view it can be understood how in his burning home to a certain man the only thing of supreme value might be the portrait of a dead, adored wife of blessed memory, and how push to the rescue of it might set fear at naught. So much would hunger to feed his urgent love of her on the mere picture of her vanished beauty and charm thrust him fiercely into flames.

Thus it is evident that the problem of courage on levels higher than instinct is the problem of building up these acquired mechanisms, whose pushes will override all aversions, all fears within, all difficulties without; that will make the bearing up against discomforts, pains and disasters possible and inevitable.

There is one type of sentiment, of various levels lower and higher, that is very much in evidence in the matter of courage. This type is generally known as honor. The name covers many varieties. It is what a man saves through perils. "All is lost save honor" is with us a great saying.

Now honor is a general name for certain forms of the sentiment of self-regard. This sentiment has as its back bone, or center of structure, the instinct of self-assertion, which instinct as previously remarked, seems well nigh to be identified with the very essence of life — life ever pushing to continue to be and to expand. But all depends not only on the push as such, but on the idea of one's self which is pushing into realization. It may be that of the mere fighting man, that of the village wrestler, the pugilist, or the duellist, who win honor in the ring, and rescue it from loss in face of any danger wherever challenged. These men are very sensitive as to what they call their honor. Which means not so much their skill in battle or their fame, though both surely are involved, as for their mastery of fear. They are not afraid, they would let you know. They may be beaten, quite likely, but they fight the more strongly, courageously. They lose perhaps the victory, but they save their honor. They face the perils of disaster without flinching. They bring out of the ring an unimpeachable self-regard as a stalwart fighting man. This form of honor has become discredited in civilized lands. Characteristically it holds its place among the aristocracy of militaristic Germany, and among pugilists, and schoolboys elsewhere.

On higher levels in an ascending series are the honors of professions, in practice of which dangers must be faced and instinctive and other fears overcome. The self regarded as of the highest importance, to be asserted, and to be realized when occasion offers, is in the line of what is named duty. That is what his *calling* calls for in the matter of conduct and mental attitude. The fireman extinguishing fires and making rescues, the policeman arresting the armed outlaw or facing the raging mob, the lifesaver putting off in an angry sea to the wreck, the trained nurse going, even preferring and eager to go, to the tending of the most malignant cases, have each his or her peculiar high sentiment of honor, of regard for a self that in their honorable calling pushes them through perils of many personal private losses, and even of death. Their courage is not that of an instinct of pugnacity, though that in a modified form is involved, nor is it that of the vigorous action of their instinct of self-assertion, though that is surely there and aggressive. It is that sentiment whereby one regards himself as a member of a body whose behavior is of this sort as a matter of course. Without that sentiment few could face such situations at all and face them so well. With that sentiment it is not so difficult. It may even come to be "all in the day's work," as King Humberto said when shot at by an assassin. That is what is to be expected in a man in the profession of kingship, as it is in another man in that of policeman or coastguard, or a woman as nurse.

Thus to enlist in a certain regiment is to put one's self in the way of developing in one's self the peculiar sentiment of honor belonging to that regiment. To be à member of the Kaiser's Imperial Guard, of the Cold Stream Guard of England, of the Scotch Greys, of the Fighting Sixty-Ninth, is to enter into possession of a mental structure. It starts to develop the instant decision to enlist is made, and increases in complexity, solidity, and vigor of action as drill, and intimate companionship with comrades increases. It is not only one's own honor, as that of a fighting man on a lower level, that moves to overriding fear. It is even more than that, the honor of the regiment that urges the man on in the face of perils.

In all these cases it should be observed, where there is a sentiment of honor in action, as in the case of inborn mechanisms, two things are involved. There is on the one hand the mechanism itself; on the other, there is the idea of the object, the stimu-

lus, which sets the mechanism going. There would
be no action however clear the idea without the
mechanism, as there would be no action of the
mechanism without the idea. It is like the piano
and the pianist. The most expert performer without his instrument is helpless, as the most perfect
instrument without the performer is useless. It
requires the presence of both for the production of
the music. So in a sentiment the degree of perfec-
tion of the idea and that also of the mechanism
which the idea sets going, determine not only that
there be action, but the quality and force of the
action, which will be awakened by the idea. Let
us take the case of a recruit who may happen to
come into battle without a trace of the sentiment
which the members of the regiment possess. On
the lower plane of courage in which the inborn mechanism of pugnacity by itself is working, he may
fight with the best of them. But if at any time his
flight mechanism should be suddenly and violently
aroused, there would be no check on its panic action,
if the terror should be strong enough to override
the anger or rage of battle. But with the members
of the regiment, there would be active not only the
instinct of pugnacity, but the sentiment of the
honor of the regiment. It is this which balked by the
enemy arouses strongly their fighting spirit, which
fighting spirit issues not only out of the inborn
mechanism of pugnacity, but also out of the acquired sentiment of the honor of the regiment. It
is the maintenance of this honor which steadies

them in the battle, more massively overrides fears, and carries their standard, the outer symbol of their inner sentiment, forward in the storm. The regiment may yield ground, where necessary. It is not likely to run in panic.

Some endeavor should now be made to analyze the constituent elements that go to the making of such a sentiment, and also to describe the manner in which they may be built into the structure.   In neither can completeness be expected, nor for our present purpose is it necessary. Something like what occurs may be suggested.

The honor of the regiment as a fighting organization will be the example used in the analysis. There of course will be present the mechanism of fear whose activity is to be overcome. Next there is pugnacity, the instinctive mechanism which in battle overrides fear. Then there is self-assertion, the mechanism which when resisted is intensified and sets going, combines with, and strengthens in action the fighting mechanism. So far, the soldier stands alone. But as a member of his regiment his gregarious instinct is involved He is one of a company, a herd, and as such he is sensitive to the arousal of the instinct of self-subjection. It is not so much the commanding officer as merely another man, as it is the officer as representative of the herd that controls him. That control is through the general tendencies briefly named and described in a former chapter. He is made by his entrance into the regiment open to suggestion. He becomes highly suggestible to the words of command of his officer, but also to the prevailing ideas of his regiment. He also is remarkably ready to feel with and as the regiment feels. This is the general tendency of sympathy. Feeling is under the dominion of regimental ideas, and its waves, by contagion in daily converse, spread from man to man, and in battle submerge them all in its tide. And still further there is proneness to act as others act— the general tendency of imitation. It includes not only unconscious doing as the herd does, but may also the conscious readiness to copy characteristic ways of behavior. In all these ways the activity of the specific mechanism of gregariousness opens the individual soldier to the action of the general tendencies molding his ideas, his emotions, his behaviors into the likeness of the regiment. To this will be added the more specific instinct of companionship, comradeship.

But underlying all this is the working of the tendency, the push to formation of habits, that is to the retention and fixing of certain ways of action in thought, emotion, conduct. Without the habit-tendency there could not be any building of structures whatever. Temperament may also be involved. Certain men, who are so built by inborn structure as to make them material that cannot be built into men possessed of the sentiment of the honor of the regiment, will be excluded from its ranks. Those of such temperament as can be so incorporated will be selected.

Doubtless other original mechanisms may be involved. But sufficient has been done to make plain what is a sentiment and how formed out of which issues courage on a higher than instinctive level. Attention, however, may be called to the presence of the protective, which is an extension of the parental, instinct. The comrade in need of help, whether hard pressed by the enemy, wounded, or even when dead, will be assisted, rescued, borne off to safety, or to honored burial.

As to voluntary methods by which these sentiments are built up, whether with consciousness of what is really being done or without, something will be said in a later chapter, on training for courage.

It may now be presumed that it has been made plain, how higher forms of courage as distinct from lower instinctive forms, are based on acquired complex mental structures, which have come to be called sentiments. There are increasingly higher levels of these superior courages. In following chapters some description will be attempted of some of these higher levels, and suggestion as to the nature of the very highest level of all.

CHAPTER VII

HIGHER FORMS OF COURAGE — *Continued*

IN the last chapter it was shown what a great part the sentiment of self-regard plays in the overcoming of fear, in the production of what we call courage. Now self-regard, that is regard for one's self as a person of a certain sort, is of many forms. As a mere duelling student in a German University a youth, as one of them told me, may after his first duel go strutting down street with chest out and head high in great exaltation of spirit, having proved to his student body, and to himself which is far more, that he is the sort of self held in high esteem by his particular herd. That is the sort of self he asserts, which he would realize, and which he regards as of greatest importance. The possession of such an acquired mechanism makes him very sensitive to public opinion, to approval or disapproval both by himself and by his student society. A new fear is generated by the building of this mechanism, the fear of disapproval by himself and others. A new satisfaction is also demanded, self-approval, and public praise. To avoid the one and win the other is the twofold reward of proving one's self to be that sort of self, or person. The push to satisfy that new urgent self, so built up, is like the push to satisfy one's instinctive hunger. The fear that it may go unsatisfied is a new fear. These two aspects of its push, positive and negative, may give it impelling power to override instinctive and acquired fears. Courage will depend, then, on the strength of this sentiment of regard for one's self as a student duellist.

When the student duellist fights with an opponent of another university, he fights not so much as a private man, but as a member of a society. His regard is not only for himself as an individual duellist, but for himself as representing, as embodying in himself, his university. When he strikes, his university strikes; when he wins or loses, it wins or loses. It is the honor of the university in which his own honor is submerged. Much else is exhibited in the conflict beside his courage, as, for example, his skill, his strength, endurance, ability to take hard blows, etc. But in this connection we are thinking of courage more than of aught else.

What is brought to light in this case of the student duellist is the same as that which was made evident in the member of a regiment. In each case it is regard for a self which is a corporate, not a private, individual self, a self approved by the body of which one is a member. In the same class is the parent, whether father or mother, who is impelled to defend the child, not only from the instinct of parental affection, but because in the community of which they are members parents are expected to do that sort of thing. Even though the instinctive impulse of parenthood be weak to override fear, yet regard for one's self as such a parent as will be approved by one's self and others in the community may re-enforce weak instinct, or even be substituted for it when it does not exist Then courage adequate to meet the peril may protect the child from harm.

It will be of interest to call the attention to a like psychological activity to which we do not attribute courage. In society life there is built up a sentiment of regard for one's self as a member of a certain class. We are not wont often to think of maintaining the honor of that class, though we are zealous to make sure to ourselves and others that we are of that class. It is like the soldier of the Scotch Black Watch making sure to himself and others that he is in that class of fighters. We in society life would so be regarded, would so regard ourselves as in our set. We are exceedingly sensitive to slights from members of that class, are easily angered by members of a socially inferior class that treat us as one of themselves. This is peculiar to no social stratum. From the parlor maid who regards herself as superior to the maid of all work, through the wholesaler and his wife who look down on the retailer, the banker whose self is to him of higher quality than the tradesman, the man of leisure whose father left him for idleness money made in selling soap fat or calico, who condescends even to bankers and manufacturers in honest big business;

through parasitic women who do nothing but spend foolishly the money of their husbands and ancestors, save to play bridge and give dinners in exchange for dinners of the right sort given by those of the approved set, up to dukes' daughters who will associate on terms of equality only with dukes' sons, and kings who see to it that they go out first to dinner, and march first in all processions, the same thing is in evidence — a zealous regard for one's place of honor in the social scale. The strong maintenance of this social position, though it is the upholding of one's self-approval, and the approval of one's set, is never thought of as courage. Yet the maintenance of one's self-regard and the regard of others as approved by student duellists, or as approved by the members of the regiment, or army, is called courage. The reason is that in these latter cases fear is overcome, as it does not seem to be in the former cases.

But attention is called to this matter because, if we do not call the vigorous maintenance of our social position courage, we do find that this attitude of mind is the basis of what we recognize as a very pronounced form of cowardice. We are immensely afraid of loss of social standing. And this is not merely an aversion to an unsatisfied push for private and public approval, as we are averse to hunger unsatisfied or sleep denied. It is surely that and beside the instinct of fear itself may be vigorously awakened, with many of its characteristic bodily and emotional activities. We may turn pale, tremble, be paralyzed for a time, feel our hearts, as we say, sink within us, when we are confronted with loss of our society standing. It is in its way as uncomfortable a condition as when a physical peril confronts us. One in such a situation feels like the duellist who has refused to fight, the soldier of a famous regiment who has flinched in battle and has lost regard for himself, as others have lost regard for him, as being one of the approved famous class.

Now to meet such a situation of social fear does require social courage, and as well social skill. It requires a strong sentiment of your own social worth that overmasters your fear, pushes to vigorous and tactful social conflict and wins one's own regard and that of others for a social self that succeeds. One can force himself by courage and tact, which is skill, into good society as into an enemy trench. In this connection is revealed the social bully, more often a woman than a man, riding over social inferiors from whom she has nothing to fear, and whose feathers come quickly down in the company of her superiors, of whose disapproval she is greatly afraid. Here also is the social braggart boasting to her social inferiors of society associations, on which she has small claim or even in reality none at all.

But let us return to the consideration of courage in its more recognized forms — courage as the subjugation of fear growing out of a sentiment of regard for one's self; as maintaining the standard of one's fighting set, whether it be that of a student body, a regiment, or a community. It will be noticed that in all these cases the development is from the private, individual, instinctive self to a public, corporate self seeking approval, and fearing disapproval of self and others in the community. Now as the community becomes broader and comprehends a wider membership, the self disclosed to public view is regarded as more than a member of a small fragment. It becomes one of a larger circle. The student duellist stands in his own eyes and those of the world at large not as a member of *a* university, but as a member of the vast student body of the German Empire. The member of the Old Guard of France is not only a member of that guard, but of the mighty French Army. The honor he has to maintain is not that of a regiment, or a corps, but of a national army, whose glory is of ancient date and exhibited on a thousand battlefields. The spectators of his behavior are not those of his immediate circle, his regiment, or even of his corps. They are the vast army of his country. Even the brave dead are a cloud of onlooking witnesses. Still further, his country whether at home as mother, father, sister, fellow townsmen, or innumerable unknown fellow citizens he has never seen, are living noncombatant witnesses of his behavior, whose honor is involved in his own. He regards himself as such an one as should do what his country calls for from a soldier of France.

It will be clear by a moment's thought that there is in his behavior the action of a number of mechanisms. These respond to the approval of his sister, father, true love, his regiment, his corps, his town, his province, his country — a vast system of mechanisms of self-regard made up of hundreds of lesser mechanisms. They all gather and win their power through being embodied in the regard for himself by himself as one whose approval of himself voices the approval of all, not only of his friends, but of his countrymen. When such a mechanism is built up, courage of a high order has come into existence. Fears for personal safety disappear. So also do fears for the sorrows, deprivations and utter disasters that by his wounding or death are to come on wife and child afar off at home. What puts, and keeps, the machine-gun soldier in his nest to hold back the advancing enemy while his own army safely withdraws, what makes it possible coolly, steadily to face and wait for certain death, to give up hope of returning to the blessed comforts and joys of home, bringing to those dear ones how great a benediction by his presence — what puts him there, keeps him there in desperate battle to the last, which makes inevitable his own death, is this vast massive complex of pushes built into a powerful drive that insures his self-approval of that which country will approve. "It is sweet and beautiful to die for one's country," sang the Roman poet. To be sure in the thick of the struggle, as in a bayonet charge, the rage of battle takes the center of the field of consciousness. Instinctive pugnacity is in violent action; to kill and yet not to be killed seems all of which one is just then aware. Yet what brought the men there, holds them there, gives mighty continuity of push in face of all terrors, is more than a rage of anger in fighting. It is this built up, acquired, and it may well-nigh be resistless complex mechanism of a regard for one's self as a patriot of England, of France or of America. Each being what each is, almost as a matter of course does what is there to be done. Till some structure of a self of this sort is built up, you do not get the higher forms of courage. You may have instinctively fierce, pugnacious men, doing brave battle like tigers, or even like angry rats at bay, or hens protecting their chicks. But you have not fighters facing the terrors of long winters in cold, wet, filthy, vermin-infested trenches, harder by far to bear than the terrors of battle, when for a time one is crazy mad with instinctive anger and its fierce hate.

In this high form of courage so issuing from a strong sentiment of self-regard there may be involved, as doubtless there is, strong fear of disapproval of self and others as well as urgent push to the satisfactions of approval. Men will vary one from another as emphasis shifts from the side of approval sought, to that of disapproval shunned. The better courage, better in point of merit not only, but of efficiency in drive, will be that in which approval rather than disapproval is emphasized, since the push is positive to achievement, and not negative to avoidance of loss.

This consideration brings into view a danger to which courage is exposed, when based on too narrow a sentiment of regard for self as upholding the standard of an organization like a regiment or army, or that of a social group such as a body of students or army officers. The danger is, through fear of disapproval by self and others as a member of a minor group, one may become a coward in face of situations of wider and deeper import. The student duellist may be afraid to refuse to fight a duel in violation of the conventional student standard, though as a kindly disposed gentleman a duel would do violence to his sentiments of courtesy and humanity. The Prussian officer's fear of violating the conventional standard of masculinity and official aristocratic superiority to the non-military man, may push him to crowd the lady off the sidewalk into the gutter, may urge him in hot anger to run through a harmless gentleman who by accident bumps into him on the street.

But still more significant and on a far higher plane is the once favorite pastime, one might almost call it, of the English officer, who, in deference to the narrow ideal of personal courage of ancient date, got himself all too easily killed. It was not to be thought of that an English officer should ask a private to face a danger he would not face himself. Prussians might do that, not he. If privates were to be brave, he more so. German officers might go behind their men. English officers were to go, if not ahead leading, at least with their men in equal exposure. It was an honorable tradition that had accomplished great results in the past. But in the conditions of the most recent warfare obedience to

it might well become and did become almost a
practical cowardice from a larger interest. It was,
in deference to a traditional standard of a group, to
sacrifice lives just then invaluable to their country,
to deprive England and her Allies of her necessary
trained officers, and, for a season all too long in a
critical time, leave her in a measure helpless. Thus,
through fear of not living up to the conventional
standard of his class, he became coward as regards
wider and more important considerations. He has,
it should be said, come to realize this, and there has
come into existence in English officer class the sentiment of a broader and wiser patriotism, whereby he
is urged carefully to save his life as the best way to
give it to his country's service. His former courage
has come to be seen to be of the nature of foolhardiness. It requires at times more courage to retreat
than to stay and fight, to run away than to stay and
be killed, saving one's private honor as a fighting
man, and losing one's country's ultimate victory,
and, more than that, its cause of justice and human
brotherhood. Thus is revealed to us a vision of still
higher courages, with their bases in sentiments of
profounder wisdom and broader fellowship. To the
discussion of these the next chapter will be devoted.

CHAPTER VIII

STILL HIGHER FORMS OF COURAGE — THE COURAGE OF DIFFERING PATRIOTISMS

IT should be quite evident now that not only are fears overcome by the development of acquired mechanisms, but new fears come into existence because of these very same acquired mechanisms. For example, consider the sentiment of gaining and accumulating wealth. This implies also the sentiment of self-regard, assertion of one's self as not only possessing, but of one's self as masterful in the gaining, the holding and the using the wealth, both in display and in still further accumulation. This sentiment gives birth to a whole group of fears of actual loss of the wealth, and so of the evidences of power; of failures to exhibit to the world through it one's self-importance. These fears are overcome by bars and bolts, by all manner of securities, whether in strong boxes or bonds. There are safes in loans as well as in vaults. There are rescues from the terrors of social obscurity bred by regard for one's self as rich and powerful by all manner of self-assertions. Thus the overcoming of fears born of the sentiment of self-assertion comes through still further development of self-assertion. It is of the very nature of the sense of power to breed timidity. In this way comes push out to increased sense of power whereby the very fears thus bred will be overridden.

Now in the last chapter we arrived at a sense of ever increasingly wide acquired structures as the basis of overcoming fear. The highly complex sentiment of love of country in the soldier with all it involved held him on the firing line, though ambition in his peaceful profession, love of wife and child, and many other urgencies pushed him from his trench. The stronger his patriotism, the more surely were his varied fears overcome, the greater, the more stable his courage. But as with other sentiments, so also with this of love of country. It brings into existence its own kind of fears, which, in turn, demand some acquired sentiment to overcome them. What mechanism must be built up to overcome the fears any given sentiment brings into existence will depend upon the nature of the sentiment out of which the fears have arisen. The meaning of this will soon appear.

At the start it should be made clear that the sentiment of patriotism, the love of country, is not always of the same character. What in any given nation it is will depend on what that nation stands for, *i.e.*, what is its essential national sentiment. If it is for the accumulation of material wealth as evidence and means of increase of material power, the domination of lands and peoples, the fears on the one hand it gives rise to, as the methods of overcoming these fears, is one thing. If, on the other hand, the national sentiment is for the establishment of the well-being of its own citizens, without prejudice to the welfare of the inhabitants of other lands, then the fears generated and the methods of overcoming them will be quite different. The qualities of courage also, it will be discovered, in the two cases will be quite different.

The most perfect example of the first sort of patriotism is exhibited to us in what we call Prussianism. Here you see a most violent, boastful and aggressive patriotism. Each true Prussian and Prussianized German is what he is because there has been built up in him the national sentiment of assertion of power in material wealth, and domination of lands and peoples. It is a sentiment more and other than economic. It involves wealth but rather as a means than as an end. National grandeur in this case is power asserted over men more than over things, though that of course is involved.

This being the central fact, we gain insight into the psychology of German fears and also into German courage. The one great dominating push of all Germans being for national power, the one great fear is on the one hand the loss of power possessed; on the other, the failure to extend the power already gained. This reveals to us what is really meant by the German claim that it was "encircled" by powers, whose existence threatened loss on the one hand and hindered expansion on the other. It has been a matter of common observation for years that Germany has been characterized by an unnecessary and to many an inexplicable fear, in spite of its manifest great and masterful power. The explanation is thus made clear. The bare existence of other countries marching on her frontiers made to her a wall against expansion. Whatever threat there was in them has been of her own making. Without the push to power of the national sentiment of her people, generating fear of her in her neighbors, there was no great cause of fear from her neighbors. Even the Alsace-Lorraine wrong she had done France had well nigh ceased to be of account to the French people, whose national sentiment as republicans had come to be, not as of yore for glory of arms and gaining of material power, but for individual well-being in matters of spirit more than in things of the body.

But still further, the sentiment of patriotism as a push to power is the mother of national envy. The evil to patriotic Germans in England was not that she threatened Germany with attack — there was not the least chance of that — but that England existed as the greatest world power. Her mere existence as such seemed to Germans, with their characteristic sort of patriotism, as an attack on their own ambition to world power. Nothing could ever appease a Germany possessed of such a kind of national sentiment, save the disappearance of England as the great world power. As that could only come to pass through the defeat of England, war against her was bound to come. Only so could the great fear of Germany that world power would be kept from her be allayed. "World power or down-fall" expresses the very essence of Germany's fear. It also will be found to express the characteristic quality of the marvellous courage of her people.

There is nothing that arouses anger, the fighting instinct, in man more quickly or more violently than the balking by resistance and still more by attack of the instinct of self-assertion. And on higher levels it is the same when offense is given to the sentiment of self-regard, especially when the self regarded is that of one's "will to power" in its various forms. As has been heretofore remarked, pugnacity is often the most active push in overcoming fear. Thus owing to the particular nature of the German's patriotism, as push to power, he has been constitutionally angry at England and all other countries that stood in Germany's way toward expansion. Education formally in school and university, and informally in press and social converse, has given expression to, and cultivated a vigorous national hate or contempt for England in particular and foreigners in general. And hate is but a sentiment of angered self-assertion, usually known as envy. It is no mean courage that has such a basis in the hate of envy. Those who are the objects of its attack are to beware of its fury.

A word in passing might be devoted to a marked trait of the German fighters. They seem to be unnecessarily and extremely cruel. The same is true of the civilian population of either sex. Their poets chant hymns of hate. Their preachers exhort to all manner of violences against innocent enemy women and children, even of neutral peoples, and whole communities of Germany celebrate the sinking of the "Lusitania," and glory in the bombing of hospitals.

So extraordinary is this cruelty of the Germans that it has been thought that they by some innate quality are different from other European races. It does not seem necessary to assume any such inborn difference. The Hessian mercenary of our War of Independence was neither so brave nor so cruel as the Prussianized Hessian, and other South Germans of today. German-Americans, not Prussianized, are characterized in this matter as are Americans of British, French or other stock. The inevitable logical inference is that this disposition is acquired, not inborn.

It would appear, then, to be quite evident that a courage arising out of a fighting disposition based on a sentiment of hate, in which a chief element is balked self-assertion, would be inevitably cruel. There does not seem to be any distinct instinct of cruelty, as is sometimes urged. Self-assertion gains its satisfaction often in destroying, annoying and causing pain. Even when merely fused with anger, and much more so when developed into the sentiment of hate, cruelty is a certainty. It may develop into a fixed habit, and so become well nigh mechanical. In domestic life we have habitual annoyers, causing discomfort and pain wherever they go, who scarcely seem to be aware of their quality. Whole

armies and the peoples back of them may have
built in their members such an acquired mechanism, as to set them on the ruthlessness of destruction
of valuables and the causing of pain quite as a matter of course. It is not itself courage, but it is the
inevitable concomitant of courage of a certain sort,
that based on self-assertion unmodified by kinder
instincts.

It can be understood then how a people, with
such an acquired basic sentiment of assertion of
power with its certain involved qualities of envy
and cruelty, will be pushed to cause fear in their
enemies, as the way to overwhelm their enemies'
courage. The method of frightfulness will seem to a
people trained into such a strong sentiment as the
obvious way of doing battle. It will not be able to
catch even a faint suspicion of the fact that the
opposite effect will be produced in a people whose
fundamental sentiment is different from their own.
As Emerson pointed out, "We find what we bring."
The stupid misadventures of German diplomatists
and her General Staff are the consequence of the
basal sentiment that has come out of the Prussia
of the Hohenzollerns. It is not instinctive to him,
but acquired, and is, as has been observed, a concomitant of a certain form of courage, which has
grave defects, as will be seen, but is as far as it goes
a courage of terrible force, and destructive and
ruthless in extreme.

There is another characteristic of the courage
springing out of this type of patriotism which should

be considered. It grows out of the emphasis that is put upon the instinct of self-subjection. The inhabitants of a country possessed of this type are subjects of a sovereign. The word "subject" is significant. They receive their laws from above. They also receive their opinions largely from the same source. Rules of behavior are dictated to them. Attitudes of mind are determined from authority. Education becomes subtly the development of a sentiment of subordination. The self that is regarded as fit and proper is one subject to the rules of etiquette, to the rules of social order from above. Conduct is hedged around by things forbidden. The paths open to instinctive or acquired self-assertion are strictly defined, and the manner of the assertion is fixed. The result is that in these paths open to self-assertion, the assertion is apt to be violent. Those in subordinate positions of authority are strongly authoritative within their restricted limits, while at the same time very subordinate to those above. So rank as such comes to be highly esteemed, and rank is determined by proper subordination in its degree. It tends to make the officer in the army and his wife, even the holder of civilian rank and wife, each a bully to his or her subordinates, of whom they can in the fixed order of things have no fear. As a matter of course this manner of asserting and feeling one's power is in and through the causing of discomfort of spirit, if not also actual bodily pain, and so is essentially cruel. Even in hospitals, it has been observed, the sensibility to feelings of the patients is to an astonishing degree lacking.

The consequence of such a sentiment of subordination is the weakening of initiative. Men become habituated to awaiting direction. Officers look to superior officers Invention must win approval from above. Thus courage of the subject tends to lack initiative, though in the line of its duty to its superiors it may be extremely strong. The machine-gun operator put in his shell-hole by his superior officer and told to stay there and kill till he is killed, whose psychological fibre is of such well-knit stuff, will stay there without a particle of doubt, unless a superior turns up betimes and tells him to clear out. To get out on his own impulse with his gun and keep himself able to go on killing, with more disastrous effect to his enemy and profit to his own army and himself, may not be possible to that sort of man thoroughly trained in subjection.

It would appear then, inasmuch as in Germany the national sentiment is one of aggressive assertion of national power as power, that courage, the push to that assertion over obstructive fears is sure to be very violent. On the other hand, it may lose in the quality of initiative, because of the strength of the correlative sentiment of subordination to the powers above of divine origin.

It is apparent that the lack of an equally strong courage in the Austrian armies with that of the Prussian is not because of inborn differences. Men are innately much the same everywhere. The difference is in the acquired structures of sentiment. It is not merely that there are many different races in Austria. So there are in the United States. It is that these different races in Austria have different racial sentiments and no unified national Austrian sentiment, like the national sentiment of Germany or of the United States. Their courage, so far as it can be active on the basis of their own various racial and national sentiments, is as terrible in battle as any courage in history. The courage of the Serbs, national brothers both racially and by sentiment of the Slovaks in the Austrian Army, is sufficient evidence thereof. Thus it is again clear that the ultimate basis of courage, giving it its quality of strength and endurance, is sentiment in the technical sense employed in this treatise. All depends on the nature of the basic sentiment.

In contrast with the German sentiment of patriotism, developed essentially on the assertion of power as power with its inevitable characteristic qualities, may be studied the sentiment of patriotism as it appears in the United States. The courage arising from it will be found to have certain different qualities, because the sentiment of patriotism in America is of a very different structure. This example of the United States is chosen rather than that of France or Great Britain, because there is found in this country a most extraordinary mixture, not only of people from different nations, but more than that, from different races, some of them of very unlike and seemingly antipathic bent. Examples are, not to mention all, Negro, Chinese, as well as Jew, Armenian, Arab, beside all of the European nationalities. Yet this war has revealed an extraordinary unanimity of sentiment, showing that whatever inborn, instinctive differences there may be, if indeed there are any, when put to the test the fundamental national sentiment is the same in all. The offer of the Chinese-Americans to enlist a regiment of their own, and other such exhibitions, and the presence of an astonishingly large number of German names in our army lists, all show that it is not race that counts fundamentally, but acquired sentiment.

Granted, then, that in America we have a single acquired national sentiment, built into the very structure of the minds of men of very different and very many races, it remains to examine its quality. As distinguished from the Prussianized German's patriotism, it will be found to be essentially a sentiment not for domination of peoples and lands, but for an order of society that makes for the well-being of men without reference to their birth or rank. Beside this, the basis of authority is not from above down, but from the people themselves. Law is not imposed upon them by another, but is self-imposed. Obedience is not of subjects to a divinely appointed emperor or king, but of citizens under a law framed by themselves, and framed for their own advantage. To be sure the realization of the ideal is far from perfect. But it is the fundamental ideal, that is the mental mechanism pushing almost as mechanically year after year as instinctive hunger pushes, to its satisfaction, or as fear pushes to escape, or anger to destroy. As German men are pushed to world power, Americans are pushed to a democratic order of society whose result is to be general well-being.

In this American patriotic sentiment are certain instinctive elements, woven into impelling strengths, that scarcely appear in the sentiment of the Prussianized German. There is to be found as its very core the tender emotion, the basis of consideration for others, without which justice, properly so called, not as efficient orderly organization for power, but as organization for help, will not exist. *Brotherhood* of the herd, not the human herd massed for power by sympathy, suggestion, imitation, but though massed gregariously as any other herd, massed by suggestion of the democratic ideal, feeling together in sympathy the same kindly disposed, helpful emotion, imitating forms of government and procedure whose outcome is general beneficence. Officers are differently disposed to their men, as the men to their officers. The push of their fundamental sentiment is toward more kindly treatment on the part of the officers, as it pushes in the men toward expectation of such treatment from those in command. There appears a new, characteristic mutual loyalty between officer, and men. To be sure it is inadequately realized here and there, perhaps far too often. But when all subtractions are made, there remains the indisputable fact that the characteristic national sentiment is there. To it state legislators and national congressmen are pushed, not only from without by the sentiment of their constituents at home, but by the inbred strong drive of this national sentiment within themselves.

There is self-assertion here of the individual as private and public person as vigorous as any to be found in a Prussian. But it is fundamentally not for power as power, but for essential right, both for the discovery of its nature and the realization of it in social order and individual well-being. When you speak of self-assertion, all depends on what kind of self is held to be of most worth, on what is the self which is pushing into being. Is it a self that is just, a democratic self, a citizen self, member of a self-governing order, or is it a governed self of a subject order, governed in the interest of the maintained and increasing material power of an autocratic small class?

There will be found no lack of the strong working of the instinct of self-subjection in this type of democratic patriotism, but it will be self-subjection to self-imposed regulations necessary to the realization of the democratic order of equal opportunity and equal justice. Obedience enjoined by civil and military officer, and given by lay citizen and private soldier, will be ultimately to the democratic ideal involved. And in this kind of self-subjection will be left large room for the free and vigorous action of individual self-assertion. There will not be the restrictions put upon it such as are found in the

Prussian order. Ranks will not be found. Fixed
artificial superiorities and inferiorities will tend to
disappear. Roads are more open for ability to win
its way. Thus initiative instead of being restricted
is given the freest play, since by it standing is
realized in a fluid society.

It is possible now to get some appreciation of the
qualities of the courage of the democratic patriot
as distinguished from that of the patriot of an autocratic order. The essence of the latter is obedience
to an unquestionable authority. It issues out of a
carefully constructed mechanism of subjection to
authority on the one hand, of assertion on the other
of national power as power. In the former case it
issues out of a carefully constructed mental
mechanism of subjection to the principle of justice,
and on the other of assertion of a social justice that
involves a private justice as the very essence of
public justice. The courage of the democratic
patriot will be on the side of instinct no stronger
than the courage of the autocratic patriot It will,
however, have greater freedom of initiative. That,
in fact, has been found remarkably true of the
American soldiers. They achieve most when left
free. Yet their freedom is never without its due and
proper measure of subordination to the general
interest, whether of the particular conflict, or to the
sacred cause of justice for which the battle rages.

But beyond any other consideration stands out
the fact that the ultimate test of the enduring
strength of an army's or a nation's courage will

reveal the moral basis of its patriotic sentiment. Here will rest at last the answer to the question of morale. It will not be in food so much, or heavy guns or multitudes of men. Other things being equal, the test will be on the moral quality of the national sentiment. And the moral quality of national sentiment will be determined by the comprehensiveness of its including all human instincts not merely, but those instincts in central position and great strength which really make in their activity toward a more insistent and steadfast courage. The seeds of decay, of deterioration of morale, of will to battle, are in a national sentiment that ignores, or subordinates to the will to power, the kinder instincts of the race. These instincts are the foundation not only of a just order, but are at last as certainly the basis of enduring national power, national wealth, and a nation's invincible courage. A courage it is not only to do battle in war, but to undertake vast, complicated reforms, and go forth in holy crusade, with no other hope of gain than in Lincoln's immortal phrase that "Government of the people, by the people, for the people might not perish from the earth."

CHAPTER IX

THE ULTIMATE FOUNDATION OF COURAGE

IT should now be very clear that courage, above the lower levels of instinct, grows out of those mental structures that by agreement are called sentiments. From these it derives its differing qualities and strengths. In the last chapter it was seen that the sentiment of patriotism is not always the same, and that the quality of courage of the patriot of different nations is not the same. It remains after brief consideration of various higher forms of courage not given any attention hitherto, to discuss the broader and profounder basis of courage, whether it be facing the difficulties of life in self-reliance, its disasters with fortitude, or its terrors with bravery. This basis of these several courages will be found to be of the nature of a philosophy of life. Some sort of philosophy, itself a sentiment, after all underlies all other sentiments, giving to them stability and energy, or sapping them of steadfastness and vigor.

But first some higher forms of courage not yet discussed. Take the sentiment of honor, in defence of which courage is so ready to appear. It has already been made evident that honor is not always the same. The honor of the duellist as a fighting man is very different from the honor of a man of his word, or the honor of a loyal friend. So also the honor of a nation seeking extension of power is far other than that of a nation seeking to establish justice. All these honors, however, have this in common, that aspersions cast on what is the pride in each, or checks on the push of the characteristic sentiment, excite anger, and may lead to blows of word or deed. In all forms honor will be asserted and defended, even in certain cases at the risk of life. And that is courage appearing in all types of honor.

But we may single out for special consideration certain high senses of honor worthy of note. An American Rhodes scholar asked by Dr. Parkin what had impressed him most at Oxford, replied, "It is this. Of the three thousand resident Oxford men every man of them would rather lose a game than win it unfairly." Here you have the honor of sportmanship. When taken into war it shows itself as taking risks, facing perils of its own creating, rather than win unfairly. A Mohammedan Saladin as well as a Christian Knight Crusader may possess it. It is a sense of honor that does not belong to the Sicilian, who, stealing up behind, stabs his enemy in the back, or the wounded German soldier who cries "Kamerad" and shoots his enemy helper. This is generally felt to be a reptile cowardice. Men with this high sense of honor do not really confess in creed nor practice in act that "everything is

fair in love and war." They dare lose the lady love
and suffer loss in battle than be unfair. They will
not bomb hospitals and hospital ships, nor treacher-
ously entrap by flag of truce and kill an enemy, even
though it would profit their country so to do.
Beyond the strong faith that in the long years to
come profit may lie with the nation that fights fair
and humanely, is the sense of self-respect that holds
a man from being dirty in sports, sneaking and
treacherous in battle, though he personally and his
club or country might profit thereby. Better die
than lose one's self-respect is his high courage.
This is the sentiment of regard for a self of lofty
quality, the product of a type of civilization that
develops men, rather than beasts of prey.

Next may be named the class of brave men and
women, whose high sense of honor keeps them in
direst perils, and through extreme weariness face
to face with disgusting erruptions of loathsome disease, the horrors of laceration and agony, minister-
ing to the sick and wounded, whether as surgeon,
assistant, or nurse. To fight in the wild excitement
of the battle line would be not only a relief, but a
joy, for delight of battle is thrilling in intensity and
quality. But to risk life just as certainly, hard up
against the firing line without battle's fierce excitement is to have courage indeed. And beyond this
through sympathy to partake of the agony one would
relieve, and to escape which one is violently impelled
by strong push of instinct, and yet to stay bearing
it, enduring through it, speaks of a courage of a

very high order. Impossible it would be unless for a
sentiment of honor carefully built up, in which the
tenderer instincts hold a large place. In battle-
courage they cannot so well appear. In the courage
of the hospital they play a great part. Other members of this class are also the stretcher bearer, the
ambulance driver and all whose part is not to have
direct part in fighting, and who, in peril of battle,
have not the relief of giving blow for blow.

In all these forms of honor, with the accompany-
ing and inevitable courage, is revealed a sentiment
of regard for a self of a distinguished character.
Two characteristics may be found in them, the
sense of fair dealing whose higher form is justice, and
the sense of humanity which involves always kindly
feeling, and which is named mercy. It will be recalled
that in discussing the differing courages of the
Prussian and American patriot, it was found that
the essential difference was in the absence of both
these elements in the Prussian, and the presence of
them both as basic in the American. Indeed, they
are to be found equally in the Briton and the French-
man as they are in the American, as the progress of
the great war has made increasingly evident. Each
is fighting for the same end, not for domination of
power, but for the establishment in control of men's
affairs of these sentiments of justice and humanity.
Power there is surely to be, but the power is of right
in justice and love, not of the right of might.

The remark was there made that the courage
issuing out of these sentiments would prove in the

long run to be more enduring, of a braver quality, and less likely to deterioration. The upbuilding of these sentiments appears to be the way of safety, of man's security and ultimate hope of salvation from all evils of war and of social decay. This brings us in sight of the deep foundations on which at last the courage of a democratic people must rest. It is a foundation on which all courage to live and to do of the private person as well as the citizen must ultimately be based. It must grow out of a powerful sentiment of justice and of humanity, which we are wont also to call love.

But that such a sentiment can come into existence in men, and be maintained in existence through the shocks of disappointments and disasters of life, depends on the existence of an ultimate faith as regards the nature of the world order. If the world be so constituted as to favor the organization of power in ruthless disregard of the claims of justice and humanity, who will be able to be brave in battle for a losing, even for at the very start a lost cause? If, on the other hand, the foundations even of power itself are felt at last to rest on justice and humanity, and that no enduring material power and prosperity can be built save in the establishment of the sentiments of justice and humanity in the minds of men, then courage to battle desperately and to the death for the building and maintaining those sentiments is possible, and it is possible only on the existence of this fundamental faith. It is a faith that need not be explicit and conscious. Oftener

than not doubtless it is implicit, and those who live
upheld in life's affairs by its existence are unaware
of the foundation on which they securely rest. Not
until some shock destroys that hidden rock do they
discover what was that which supported, comforted,
gave them courage to bear and dare.

This faith is of the nature of a religion. It may
be as vague and impersonal as Matthew Arnold's
sense of a "tendency that makes for righteousness,"
or as definite and precise as an anthropomorphic,
manlike deity of orthodox Christians, or Moham-
medans, a God creating things to be as they are.
Such a definite faith can sing with Pippa:

> "God's in his heaven,
> All's right with the world."

Or say in words put into the mouth of Mazzini in
the darkest hours of his endeavor:

> "I have seen past the agony:
> I see God in Heaven and strive."

But whatever be its form, its essence must be a felt
assurance that things favor right, or courage to
fight to uphold it ceases to be possible. No man can
long keep at building a house of sand on the sea-
shore, or writing his name in water. He must feel
that the work of his hands is going to stay, that the
order of things guarantees and upholds it in existence. He cannot believe that the issue of his battling
is agony. Beyond the agony he must see that for
which he struggles surely rising into being.

If, on the other hand, the order of things in violence of all sense of humanity and justice upholds and guarantees the persistent and increasing extension of material power, then sustained courage to resist it becomes impossible. The "Good God" of the Kaiser, whose throne is not as the Psalmist contends justice and right, but is irresponsible and irresistible power, makes the cause of democracy a lost cause before battle for it begins. The world cannot ever be made "safe for democracy," when the push of the great world is not only against it, but for the establishment of its contradictory opposite. So at last our courage both for its quality and its strength rests on an ultimate faith, which is, as has been remarked, of the very nature of religion.

Striking illustrations of the immense driving power of such a faith are abundant in history. From the Roman Christian Legion, renowned for extraordinary bravery, conquering under the standard of the Cross, through Cromwell's Ironsides strong in a sterner faith, and Americans battling for justice singing "John Brown's *body* lies a-mouldering in the grave, but his *soul* goes marching on," to the French Revolutionaries, who, without any belief in or hope for a life of reward hereafter, as has been nobly said, "went to their graves as lightly as to their beds for a dream of a nation's liberty," — all these were brave exceedingly in the faith, that at the heart of the world were forces strong for and not against their high and holy cause. And the trend of man's endeavor and man's achievement, slow in results though that endeavor be, and all too small the achievement, seems surely to give grounds for justification of that faith.

Perhaps even more astonishing in its quality is the courage of those few great souls who have grown into a sentiment of high regard for what becomes a man as a man. They are able to confront a soulless iron universe of mechanical law, without flinching, as proclaiming here is something still greater, even more worth while. It reveals an immense self-respect which such a man, godlike, in a godless universe, will not lose, will assert in the face it may be of no approving audience but himself. To commit suicide with Cato, discouraged by disaster, would be to show cowardice, would detract from the proper dignity and greatness of man. The counsel of Cicero to a friend, "to hope for the best issue, be prepared for the hardest, and bear whatever is to happen," is the fitter part for man to play in a hostile world. Such a courage, if not based on a sustaining philosophy of the Universe, is surely, nevertheless, built on the strong foundation of a philosophy of man — of man who is still the child of this universe, and the greatest of its offspring, and whose mere existence contradicts implicitly this sternest of creeds.

One more example and the last of high courage. It is that arising from a strong sentiment for a most sacred cause, together with that from an equally strong sentiment of a lofty self-regard, that is regard for a self as invincibly loyal to that cause. The cause seems lost, but a last perilous, desperate endeavor may perchance save it. Who knows? It is worth the adventure. There is here the courage of despair. At the worst, there is no more than the failure that already exists. To survive the lost cause without first staking all is not for the upholders of that cause. Self-regard would then be lost, and it is not to be thought of that one should live with honor gone. If at last through the perilous adventure life should survive, though the cause go down, self-regard would have been saved. Thereafter life could be endured, with vain regret to be sure, but without shame, though also without hope. The supreme test would have been met on the battle-field, and would still be faced with daily contempt for the cowardice which would crawl away from heroic endurance into the unconsciousness of death.

CHAPTER X

Training for Courage in General

It may now be taken for granted that one thing has been made evident. It is that for every form of courage higher than that of instinct, some modification of inborn structure has taken place. On the level of instinct we saw that the inborn mechanism of fear is overriden by some other inborn mechanism, more often than not by pugnacity. When we go beyond this, some modification of inborn structure takes place. This may take the form (1) of fixing instincts which are by nature variable in some particular habitual form of behavior, (2) of forming habits of action by instincts working in combination, (3) of building them into those organized systems which it has been agreed to call sentiments in a technical sense previously expounded. In all these cases we have at work the principle of habit formation. In the second and third cases the principle of push to unification into organized systems appears. In the third comes into view the principle of rationality, whereby the push is to structure of ideas around which the unification of instinctive emotional and motor elements is accomplished.

This being so, the problem of building up courage above instinct is first of all the problem of forming habits, and next of the structure of sentiments. How can these habits be formed, these sentiments be built in a man by himself or by others? This is our concern in the present chapter.

There are some general principles involved that should at the start be described. First, in the formation of habits there are two laws at work. They have been named the "law of exercise," and the "law of effect." What is meant may be made plain by the simple example of hammering a nail. The strokes at first may fall anywhere except on the head of the nail. By repetition of strokes all those that fail to hit are at last eliminated, and that kind of stroke which is effective, which succeeds in producing the desired effect, hitting the nail head, remains. In this illustration the two laws named above appear: exercising, that is, repeating the strokes, and effecting successful hits are both necessary to form the habit of hitting nails on the head. Both are summed up in our adage, practice makes perfect. But these laws explain how it is that practice makes perfect. No matter what we undertake to do, ride a bicycle, play the piano, paint pictures, write books, practice medicine or law, do business, or even govern an empire, these two laws hold.

It will be observed that there are two agreeable feelings involved in these activities of repetition and success. Exercise of itself, the mere doing whether of body or mind, is agreeable. And beside, that doing which is successful is in addition agreeable. We like to play games though we lose. We like to win also, because if for no other reason, we succeed in our doing. There are to be sure other reasons why we like to win, but we need not mention them here. A man may keep busy for hours shooting at a mark. He is doing and would succeed in his doing, gaining at least one pleasure, it may be two. These agreeable feelings play a great part in man in fixing his habits.

The action of habits at first thus formed afterward is performed increasingly in a mechanical way, until it comes to be done largely without consciousness both of guidance and also of agreeable feeling. This forming of habits is the basis and meaning of all drill of body and mind, whether undertaken by one's self over one's self, or by one's self over others.

The Duke of Wellington once exclaimed, "Nature! Habit is ten times nature." Nature as inborn, unorganized mechanism is not to be depended upon. These mechanisms may go off at any time in undesirable ways with disastrous results. It is only as these are fixed by habit to act in certain situations in a well-nigh mechanical, inevitable way is there safety. Thus fear situations that by instinct cause flight may by training come to cause attack. A different motor response is made to follow than the instinctive one. So by drill there may be substituted for all instinctive situations of fear other actions than flight actions. The actions belonging to other instincts can be tied firmly to disgust or fear. The

sensitive nurse before disgusting wounds acts from
pity, not disgust. The timid man before a danger
acts from instincts of self-assertion, or anger, or
parental affection, not from fear. When these acts
of other instincts than fear are by drill securely and
permanently attached to fear situations, you get the
courage of habit, which is for permanence and
strength ten times habit. By drill you fortify a man,
past all likelihood of change, against relapse into
instinctive action. By drill you strengthen ever
more and more the connection of the substituted
action in place of the inborn one.

All possible situations of fear, so far as discovered
by actual experience, or imaginable by forethought,
must have attached to them fixedly other forms of
action than the inborn instinctive ones. And until
this is done, a soldier in face of new situations of
peril is like the pugilist confronted by a new blow
of his opponent, he has not yet an established
mechanism to meet it. In such a case the action may
be unseemly and disastrous flight. Native instinct
acts, when a substituted form of action is not at
hand.

In confused consciousness, when a man sinks to
instinctive levels of existence, these habits being by
nature artificial connections are broken up and
inborn mechanisms are apt to hold sway. Thus
training has to be of habits of thought, of intelligence. A man must be so firmly organized in habits
of thought, as well as in those of act, that in difficult
and strange situations he may keep and not lose

his head. He keeps them above and well out of the level of instinct, and habitual action follows intelligence, and native impulse is supplanted by acquired mechanism.

So far habit in its more simple forms has been considered. But habit on higher levels than of simple combination of instincts is yet to be discussed. The second principle involved in training for courage is that which appears in the upbuilding of those mental structures which are called sentiments. Here appears a fact open to observation and which Ribot states as follows: "An idea which is only an idea, a simple fact of knowing by itself produces nothing, does nothing, it only acts if it is *felt*, if it awakes tendencies, motor impulses.[6]" That is to say, the putting of thoughts into the head as bare thoughts effects nothing. They must awaken emotions and motor activities of body. And this can come to pass only as there is built up a mechanism of emotion and action that the ideas can set going. It would be like the case of a typist without a machine. Nothing would be done. A tennis player cannot be trained off a court by lectures. For what is a tennis player but a mechanism of mind and body set up to act in certain fixed ways in face of certain situations? By practice he adds more and more fixed ways of meeting more and more new situations. He is beaten when situations occur for which he has no corresponding mechanism or habit set up. He is forever learning, that is fixing, new habits to meet the new plays of his opponents.

It is the same in the case of the man of honor, with this difference that emotions are involved in a way and to an extent that may not appear of necessity in a tennis player as such. Without such training in emotional habits a man cannot respond to ideas of honor. No appeal can be made to such a man. The bare ideas by themselves "do nothing, produce nothing." Training is, then, not only in imparting ideas, the stimuli, but also in building up the mechanism of emotion and action which these ideas, the stimuli, set off into performance. Only as there has come into existence this mechanism can ideas "do *something*, produce something." But the something that the ideas are to produce is other and more than emotion. It must be deeds. When emotions by themselves are produced we have sentimentality. There is thus revealed a marked difference between sentimentality and sentiment. In the former, the action produced by ideas stops with emotion; in the latter, it passes on, reinforced and heated, into action. It will be recalled that social instincts, those inborn mechanisms named and described in Chapter III, had their three parts: the knowing, the emotional and the motor or doing parts. It is the same with these structures technically called sentiments. They also have the same three parts. Any acquired structures that have not all these same three parts in their action are not technically sentiments. They may be acting as mere ideas, or as mere sentimentalism. In sentiment the idea arouses emotion and action.

How, then, are we to build up these structures of sentiment, whose action in certain situations gives us courage on increasingly higher levels as has been shown? From what has just been said putting mere ideas by themselves in the head is of small importance. This is why wise precepts fall dead. Also arousing emotions alone by themselves, by song and story, by play and preaching of itself makes no bravery. Soft characters, easily cowards in face of danger, come by that road. There are required ideas to be sure, therefore teachers of ideas. There are required also arousements of emotion as surely, and therefore preachers, but beyond this are required drillmasters who put ideas and emotions into action. That is how those mental structures are built up without which courage of a high order will not appear.

Fortunately, social life from infancy up is, unknown to us, a school in which we get ideas, emotional incitement, and are required to turn thought and feeling into action. But this school far too often is not stern enough in its discipline. In it we are not subject enough to severe training of thought and emotion put into action. There is needed for most of us the presence of the drill sergeant, stern of mien and inflexible in command, who sees to it that we do not stay idle dreamers, or sentimental feelers, but stout doers. That drill sergeant may be one's self, a parent, a friend, or better, a company, a brotherhood, a party, a church, a cause, in which one enlists to hold certain true ideas, experience certain high emotions of "admiration, hope and love," and put them valiantly into action. Said the poet Whittier — The best advice he could give a young man was this, that he should find some unpopular righteous cause, mount his horse and ride to enlist in it. "Enlist" is the significant word. "Whatsoever things are honorable, of good report. . . . Think on these things." That is well to be sure. Daily reading of some scripture of high import is well. But it is not enough. Attendance on arousing meetings whether they be political, patriotic, or religious, that too is well, but that still is not enough. You must enlist and that means for action. All are necessary for the structure within you of those vigorous mechanisms which go out into conquering action when the hour of fear comes upon one.

It is a great day for the young society girl or for any woman when she offers herself for training as nurse. Before that of unbalanced refined feeling, avoiding disgusting sights and overafraid of creeping things, and of contagions on street car or in crowds, she soon thereafter becomes strong to help though sights disgust and fears waylay. She goes about her professional task not indeed unafraid, but *though* afraid. So it is a great day for a young man when he sets himself to disagreeable and none-too-safe undertakings. From the mollycoddle of his home and set of social idlers, he straightway finds himself transformed into a man indeed.

So far the modes of training involved have not

been formal and systematic. They have been such as are to a great degree unconscious to those whom social converse, whether by personal contact or otherwise, is transforming. And even when conscious it has not the organized, systematic character that is found in schools or armies. It remains to consider each of these. Leaving to the next chapter the training in courage peculiar to the soldier in an army, we have here to consider the attempt systematically in school and university to build up sentiments, the outcome of which shall inevitably be courage.

Perhaps the best example of the systematic building of a sentiment, which results of necessity in developing courage, is patriotism. How as matter of history such a systematic training in patriotism in school and university has been accomplished, is given us in shining example by Germany. After the disasters of the battles of Jena, Eylau, and Friedland in 1806, when the Prussian Kingdom well nigh ceased to exist as an independent nation, and when all Germany became tributary to the Napoleonic Empire, there was undertaken the deliverance of Germany from this intolerable situation. There existed no patriotism of Germans for Germany. Germans had no courage to resist their conqueror and fight against his victorious armies from France. Courage had to be made, and the courage needed, it was felt, could only spring from patriotism, and patriotism we have seen is a sentiment, not only of ideas, or of emotions, but of ideas and emotions

incarnate in trained actions. And to create that
sentiment of patriotism was the task of certain
great Germans of that time. Only one of them was
Prussian. But they found in Prussia, a then small
part of the German people, a center of compact
organization from which to do their work. The
greatest of these men, Baron Von Stein, stated their
purpose as follows: "We started from the fundamental idea of rousing a moral, religious, patriotic
spirit in the nation, of inspiring it anew with courage,
self-confidence, readiness for every sacrifice in the
cause of independence of the foreigner, and of
national honor.'" They organized a system of training, imparting ideas, arousing emotions, drilling in
action in disguised forms, till beaten and cowed
Germany arose with tremendous courage against the
foreign strong tyrant, and in the War of Liberation
of 1813 and 1814 drove him and his hordes across
the Rhine. The story of it is most interesting and
profitable for instruction as to what may be done
and how done in restoring to independence and
courage a defeated, despairing, downtrodden people.

The lesson of this deliverance through systematic
training in patriotism has not been lost. It has been
taken up as a conscious, carefully planned and
rigidly carried-out system of education, first in
Prussian, and afterwards in all German schools.
Today we see the consequences of it in the present
"School-made War,[8]" with its astonishing exhibitions of courage of an entire people in facing, without recoil for more than four years, not only the

terrors of battle, but the hungers, the deprivations of all sorts, and the sorrows of death that have agonized every household in the land. It will be apparent how this method, so nobly born, has been for more than a half century perverted to the development of a national sentiment of power for power's sake, involving envy and hate, with their concomitants of frightfulness and ghastly cruelty.

May not a hint be taken from German experience? May not other peoples, French, English, Italian, American, as well be systematically trained, better than has been done in looser informal ways, into a democratic patriotism very different from an autocratic one? Particularly in America is such a systematic training into a democratic sentiment necessary, where we have coming to us peoples of many races from many lands. They come often with sentiments of patriotism for the lands of their birth that persist, though their native lands have been left, perhaps through antagonism to that for which those lands stand. Our schools, from kindergarten up to university, for pupil and instructor alike, should be centers of training, for building up the democratic sentiment, the sentiment not only of equal opportunity for personal and private self-assertion, which far too often is that for which America stands, but for equable distribution and possession of all the goods of life whether material or spiritual. This sentiment, deeply based, and strongly woven of ideas, emotions, and acts, will dispose our people to sacrifices of property, of personal ambition, to

facing all manner of discomforts, and dangers, and
even death itself for something dearer and more
sacred to man than power and dominion and the
glory that comes of them. There would be dominion,
but of the reign of right. There would be glory, but
of the triumph of well-being in spirit, and, as inevitable consequence, possession of all those other
goods which come with, and because of justice, and
are abundant for all in proportion as right prevails.

The methods of this formal training in school and
university should be with us, as it has been in
Germany, first of all through the teaching of national
history. But it should be the teaching of American
history as embodying a movement, progressive and
to a great degree conscious, toward the establishment of political and social justice. Carlyle wrote,
"The proper Bible of a people is its own history."
For peoples of England, France, America, who,
whatever may have been their past endeavor, are
now consciously set toward a moral democracy,
Carlyle's saying is profoundly true. In the teaching of such a history in our universities there should
be free criticism of it, where that movement has
gone astray. But that criticism should be at once
sincere and loyal to its essential spirit. In some of
our leading universities there are professors of
history, who, in a spirit of levity and cynicism, set
themselves to dressing down the Fathers, turning
to ridicule their irrelevant idiosyncracies and petty
vagaries, and thus obscuring for their students what
was the essential heroic spirit and achievement of

those who left us a great and sacred heritage. The teaching in our schools should be by song and story, by fervor of speech, and by some form of practical doing, by which our youth should be enlisted as champions of this cause of justice, for which America has to some extent stood in the past, is now valiantly standing, and is more to stand in the future. Thus, though the method is that of Germany, the cause, for the furtherance of which it is applied, is far different. It is not for the expanding of a material power, to the advantage of small aristocratic and commercial classes, but for the framing of such an order of society, in which the profiting of any one of us necessitates the profiting of all of us.

And for training into action, of ideas that by themselves do nothing, of emotions that stopping short of deeds become sentimental, it may be well considered if military training to a certain degree may not have a great value. The boy scout movement implies it. Such training develops group action, comradeship, obedience, subordination to an ideal. It brings home to the growing youth, and and to the foreign-born man, the sense of obligation that the rights of American democracy involve and necessitate. As so used it is not militarism, but its antithesis. It is preparation to keep democracy safe by trained skill in upholding the rule of equal right by strength of arms, against misrule at home, or attack of ambition of power from abroad. It would be a brave people indeed so trained into invincible power in the cause of justice and humanity.

How brave these allied peoples in that cause already are! For how much more might their bravery have counted if they had been more adequately prepared to uphold their growing democracy, and crush the attack made upon it by an arbitrary "will to power"!

Concerning the manner and value of military training as such, as creating courage, discussion will be found in the following chapter.

CHAPTER XI

The Conditions and Special Training of Soldiers for Courage

In the last chapter were described in detail the methods of acquiring habits and of building those structures called sentiments. It will not be necessary to repeat what has been said there. The same laws of psychic life will be present in the more special training of the soldier.

Much emphasis was laid in that chapter, and indeed throughout this whole treatise, upon the great part these sentiments play in making men courageous. There are, however, certain happenings that seem to falsify this conclusion. For example, in the first Battle of Bull Run in the Civil War, the men in the Northern Army must have possessed strong sentiments of patriotism. They were eager to preserve the Union. Many of them also went into the ranks pushed by desire to remove the ultimate cause of that war, slavery, and by the sentiments of justice and mercy for the colored man. Yet they broke and fled in wild panic, without any proper cause for such action. Evidently sentiments of patriotism and of a just cause are not enough. What was the matter? What was lacking? It is replied that they were raw troops, not sufficiently trained. What, psychologically speaking, is meant by raw troops? And what psychologically is sufficient training? Let us endeavor to get a clear understanding of such occurrences, and of what are the elements involved.

To accomplish this we go back to a restatement of what has often before been noted. We have on the one hand an outside thing, object, or situation, say an enemy soldier, an attacking outflanking hostile army, or some one of many other fearsome things. On the other hand we have psychic mechanisms in the soldiers facing this fearsome attack. These mechanisms are set going in a certain way, and the soldiers take flight in panic. The problem then is twofaced: either to change the situation outside the soldiers, or to change the mechanism inside them. In fact, often both have to be effected. In the history of warfare courage has been brought into being by doing both often at the same time. Let us study first the outside change. David, with his sling as against Goliath's long, heavy spear, "like a weaver's beam," changes the outside situation and he is made thus secure against panic fear. In the course of history we can see the spear of Goliath made into a javelin, which is a thrown spear, then into an arrow. So, also, David's slung stone becomes a bullet, a cannon ball, outshooting for distance and accuracy the Goliath giant on the other side. Thus fighters became courageous by changing the fearsome situations they had to con-

front. On the side of defense, as well as that of
attack, conditions for courage were made by invention of shield and armor, by walls of cities and forts,
by armored ships, by trenches and barbed-wire
entanglements, by alert sentinels ever awake and
quick to observe and report. So by their fortresses
and their arms and munitions peoples do away with
their fears, sleep quietly o'nights and go with sense
of security about their daily affairs. It all comes by
changes wrought in the outside. Fearful situations
by changes in them lose their power to excite fear.

But there are many not so obvious changes that
have to be made in these outside situations to assure
courage in fighting men, and fortify them in it.
A few of the more important may be described.
There is the whole matter of supplies which must
be at hand when needed, food, clothing, arms and
ammunition for the same. For a time soldiers may
stand firm, poorly clad and fed, and with too few
and too ineffective arms, and scant and poor ammunition, but only provided they are assured that these
things are not far off and are in abundance sufficient
for their need. Should the situation show them
non-existent, or far too few, courage of even the
best troops is likely to give way. In the Russo-
Japanese war at a certain battle the two armies at a
critical place and time confronted each other, with
ammunition exhausted on both sides. For the
moment they plucked up clods of earth and flung
them at each other. Ammunition for the Japanese
arrived. The Russians broke and fled. Had it come

to the Russians instead, the break would have been on the other side. Thus, equipment, commissary, and ordnance departments, well organized and highly efficient, are elements in the outside situation of the very greatest importance for the maintenance, as well as the very existence of courage in soldiers. It is a common and very regrettable error, one that is traditional and foolish, to regard the quartermaster and the ordnance officer as of inferior standing to the fighting man on the line. Many victories are won rather by the supply than by the fighting corps. The forward ranks of so-called combatants are there and doing well, because of the courage that is given them by the so-called non-combatants in the ranks of supply behind and up to the firing line. In modern warfare more than ever before victory rests with supply. And more often than not as able, efficient and heroic men are needed in supply as are needed at the front. A great commander is not a mere courageous fighter. He is at once a master commissary and ordnance officer. Napoleon was an extraordinary example of this, and because the commander is felt to be that to his men, guaranteeing them all manner of supplies without stint and without failure, when needed, the situation is one that sets going mental mechanisms that override fear. If these things fail, if the commander fails them, or loses their confidence, you have a situation outside which is very likely to set off the mechanisms of fear and you have a condition of things that makes for panic. To be sure he must inspire confidence in his skill as strategist and tactician, but even so, there must go with it confidence in him as organizer of supply.

So far there has been described the nature and changes made in outside situations, by reason of which the mechanisms of fear will not be set in action; or changes in situations by which mechanisms that override fear will be made to act. We turn now to consider the changes to be made in mechanisms within the soldier. We are to seek to discover what changes by training can be made in them, and what modes of training are best adapted to effect these changes, in order to give soldiers the courage to face fearful situations. Since nothing has been done, perhaps at times nothing can be done to change the outside situations, it may be something can be done with the inside mental structures, which react to these outside dangers. Just this is what all training really undertakes to do. Its object is to change inside structures to meet certain outside conditions.

This training may effect either the knowing part of these mechanisms, or the acting part of them, or again, both. By the first the intelligence in face of perils is developed. One comes to understand and by understanding controls his action. By the second one comes to acquire fixed, well-nigh mechanical, automatic ways of responding to these fearful situations. By the third a soldier becomes at once intelligent and mechanical. He understands and uses with intelligence his fixed mechanisms. He does not lose his head, nor does he lose his habits.

He is master of the situation that confronts him by virtue of this double training.

The training of intelligence is first to be considered. By a developed intelligence fearful situations may be discovered not to be fearful. And as well we discover new dangers, get to know new situations hat may bring on us loss, injury or death, also to know that we need not be afraid even in these new situations. That is to say, one changes his ideas of the objects outside. What sets off his mechanisms is not the bare object as at first perceived, but the new ideas one comes to get attached to that object. All our lives from childhood up this process goes on of learning not to be afraid of certain things and to be afraid of other things once not fearful. That means we change our ideas of them. Then the emotional and active parts of our mechanisms change with these changes of the knowing part of them. In one case, neither feelings of terror nor acts of escape occur where they were wont to occur. In the other case, both may come to happen and with violence, where without previous experience they would never happen.

For example, man has no inborn instinctive fear for all manner of firearms. He shows such inborn fear in early childhood for animals, which he later loses. In the first case, he has acquired fear, by getting ideas of these implements. In the latter case, he has lost fear through change of his ideas of them. It is said in the Kentucky mountains it is dangerous to make a motion to get your handkerchief out of your hip pocket. You may be shot on the spot, for that motion means down there reaching for your gun, so carried in that country. Better go without a handkerchief than run such risks.

Now, in modern warfare, there are thousands of situations on the face of them harmless, all of which are perilous. Those have to be learned. Learning means attaching to those situations ideas of danger and so setting off the instinctive emotions of fear and movements of escape as an inevitable consequence. These instinctive emotions and movements will need, in turn, a special training in order to their control. Just to discover new perils is to increase tendencies to terror and flight. Intelligence must be developed beyond discovery of new unexpected, sudden dangers into discovery of how to make those dangers not dangerous. Against arrow and spear the soldier puts on shield and armor, against cannon shot and shell he builds fortress and trench, against the stout enemy in front he learns to outflank. To overcome the new terrors which intelligence creates and reveals, comes increase of intelligence. So we have war colleges for the officers of ever-increasing courses of study in number and difficulty. And for the soldier of the ranks we have not only drill in fixing habits of obedience, but we also get him to add ideas to things and situations outside him. The situations outside may not change, but the ideas by training attached to them will be many, new, sometimes hard to get attached, and needing much practice to get them at hand when wanted. It is, then, ideas, intelligence, what you are trained to think and know, when confronted with certain situations, rather than the bare situations themselves that is of first importance. Ideas of one sort attached to a situation will set off the fear mechanisms; ideas of another sort will set off other mechanisms — those that will override fear. From this point of view it would seem that ideas are all. These ideas, however, of course must tend to correspond to the facts outside. You cannot knock down a fortress with your fist, even if you fancy you can. But on the other hand, you will never be able to knock it down with artillery unless you think you can. "They can who think they can," is largely true. To train soldiers to know what can be done, or even may be done, makes them able to do it, though lions be in the way. The unintelligent soldier is at a disadvantage. He does not know what can be done, and also what is equally important, he does not know what cannot be done. It is a matter of chance with him. One of the rock foundations of courage is intelligence. But the intelligence for the soldier has to be special for his profession as well as, or in addition to, a general intelligence. Soldiers who have a solid foundation of sentiments of a righteous cause that can be made to prevail, and who have beside a large general development of intellectual powers, and in addition on this basis the special training in the affairs of warfare, will become the bravest soldiers in the world.

But to achieve this they must be trained, not

only on the side of intelligence, but also on the side
of practical skill. The soldiers at Bull Run had
neither this special intelligence, nor the special
trained skill. They did not know their job. They
had general intelligence to a degree rare in armies.
They had also sentiments of a noble patriotism and
lofty ideals of justice. But these were not enough.
Later in the war the same sort of men at Atlanta,
after special training in their profession, when suddenly and unexpectedly they were attacked in the
rear by Hood's army, coolly right-about-faced and
beat off the enemy who came on confident in the
success of his surprise No matter how generally
brave one is, how generally intelligent and unswerv-
ingly loyal to high ideals, if he is not specially
trained, he cannot manœuver a battleship, and
when he discovers his helplessness, he is sure to be
overwhelmed by panic fear, and there is absolutely
no escape from the disaster of it.

It would seem, then, that other things being equal,
all depends on the special training. It is in order
now to consider the elements of this special training.
To do this will require an understanding of just
what mechanisms in man instinctive and other are
involved, how they may be controlled, and what
special drill of body and mind will bring this about.
Control is nothing else than building certain mechanisms that will act well nigh inevitably in certain
given situations, instead of other mechanisms inborn
or acquired whose action would be undesirable and
disastrous in those situations.

Courage, as was shown in Chapter IV, is largely the overcoming of fear. What other things may be involved in courage just now do not matter. It will be well to consider what in the soldier's life, especially in fearful situations, it is that excites his mechanisms of fear. It is sudden, unexpected occurrences of sight and sound, particularly very loud noises. Taken unaware, we jump, are startled by even slight movements or noises. Such a movement in the bushes or in our room, the crack of a stick on which we step or in the furniture when alone at night in the woods or in our room may at first stop one's heart and breath, then quicken them with foolish terrors for the moment. In like manner in battle, the enemy suddenly appearing where he is not expected, or a big shell exploding without warning suddenly near by, may throw a battalion of soldiers into terror before they know what has happened.

In general, then, we may say the element in a situation most likely to set off fear is surprise. It will always do it. It is as inevitable as the ringing of a well-made door bell when the button is pressed. If a soldier is as well made as the door bell, that means if his fear mechanism is in good repair, as it is sure to be in all but a few abnormal men, it will act surely, quickly and likely as not violently, when there is surprise. One thing that has to be provided against, then, in all training of soldiers for courage is surprise. To effect surprise of the enemy is the one thing his opponent tries to accomplish. To avoid it is the one thing this enemy has to achieve. A great part of danger of panic is gone when surprise is eliminated. But the surprise in situations disappears to a great extent, when one has become familiar with those situations in which surprise occurs. So training involves becoming, as we say, used to such situations. First make-believe situations of surprise have to be met. In mock-battle startling appearances of mock enemies, sudden loud explosions at unforeseen times and in unexpected places, breed familiarity. The soldier gains to some degree the attitude of expecting that almost anything may happen anywhere and at any time. Slowly and by degrees from make-believe he is inducted into real battle, before he enters self-reliant and ready for well nigh any new sight or startling sound and becomes so a veteran. So far as he is made incapable of surprise, he is to that extent delivered from *panic* fear, though not from fear altogether. That he never can be altogether trained to that point is at once the basis of his safety, as it is also the basis of his experiencing panic. He walks ever between two dangers, a narrow path between fearing too much and not fearing enough or at all. As was said before, in the brave man his fear mechanism is always in good working order, but under control, ready for surprise, but not thereby thrown into panic. To put it paradoxically, wisely afraid and therefore not afraid. That is the best courage. And training to face surprise and facing it so has that for its end.

But courage as we know is more than facing fearful situations, of which surprise is so large a part. It is also training to face hard situations. It is training in physical and mental endurance of broken rest, long marches, hard work, heavy burdens, of hunger, wet, and cold; training in fixed and continued attention, alertness of mind, intelligent thinking in many ways, special to the soldier. And this must first go forward in mock ways in training camp, then slowly in increasingly real and fierce warfare till a soldier is inured to bearing all hard things that are the part of a soldier's life. So are built up in him the mechanisms that are to act somewhat mechanically in the situations in which he finds himself. Only to a certain extent, sometimes not at all, can there be made any change in the outside situations. Beyond this, all changes by which dangers are to be met must be made within the soldier himself, in the mechanisms built up to react to those situations. The character of that training is just that which will build best these inside mechanisms which are to act just so.

But we have dealt so far first with the instinct of fear as it is affected pre-eminently by surprise; secondly, with the aversion to discomfort and to excessive effort, which is met by training into endurance. But other instincts are involved in training. The instinct of gregariousness plays in armies at battle a great part. Here arises the problem of mob action. Crowds of men behave very differently from single men, or small groups of men. It has been said,

"One is a man, several are people, many are animals.⁹" This is an exaggeration of the fact, but that an army may not of a sudden become a herd of animals or even of wild beasts, requires special training. An army has the tendency of a herd to panic, as single men have not. The reason of this is found in the action of those general tendencies briefly described in Chapter III. These are (1) the tendency to take suggestions. Men in crowds are highly suggestible. They are ready to take in and act on ideas that to them apart from the crowd would not be attended to, would be heard only to be cast aside. (2) Men also in crowds are subject to contagions of emotion, excitements of all sorts, which would not appear in a single man or in a small group, arise and spread from man to man in a crowd and are intensified by interaction. So panic fears starting with a few spread through the mass. So, also, swamping of fear, though not so easily, may take possession of a mob and all manner of things be done in lynching or destruction of property, or rough handling of the police. In this also will appear (3) imitation, the doing what others are seen doing. The action of these three things together in the herd or army, sometimes one, sometimes another, being more prominent, suggestion of the idea of an act, contagion of emotion, or imitation of an action done by others, may set an whole army running away or charging forward. The likelihood of this has been recognized by commanders as of the greatest danger, especially when coupled with, or brought into action by, surprise. Panic has been, perhaps, rather than any other cause, that which has oftenest lost battles. The problem is by some training to control this action of gregariousness. Is it not possible to use it for the advantage of the army, or at least to reduce its dangers?

In seeking a solution let it be kept in mind that crowds differ one from another, and so do armies. Men composing either may vary enormously in intelligence, and in the broader, deeper sentiments on the basis of which they act, and on which basis training may be superimposed. It has been remarked that the bravest, coolest soldiers, those most able to control fears, are those who combined with intelligence, have lofty sentiments. It is this class of soldiers who may be least subject to those psychological conditions that produce panic fears. So training for courage, even as against panics, is first of all training into a citizenship of intelligence and lofty ideals. Suggestion of ideas, contagions of emotions, or imitation of actions, contrary to, or not in harmony with their intelligence and their ideals, feelings and habitual actions, are not likely to happen to those so trained. But granted such deeper, broader training in the men who come to compose the army, what special training is necessary, and just what instincts does it train? It will be recalled that education has to find in man something that is already in him to be trained. You do not, by training, inject, as by a syringe, something not already in a man. You take hold of something born in him

and modify it or combine it with other things born
in him. What inborn elements can be taken hold
of and used to counteract these tendencies of the
herd to mob action, of the army to panic? Suggestion, sympathy, imitation will act in any case. They
will have to be made use of. But how? The answer
is in the first place by means of some other inborn
mechanisms in man, and in the second place by
building up acquired mechanisms. The herd, the
crowd has to be organized that it may not become a
mob.

To accomplish this there is one instinct more than
any other that must be used. It is that of self-
subjection. This is not fear, though there are those
who confuse it with fear. By fear among other
ways it can be brought into action, but fear is far
from the only way it can be made use of. It is
agreeable to most men to be in some ways and to a
degree in subjection to others. Most of us like
dependence. It brings agreeable feeling to nearly,
if not indeed to all of us, in certain relations. This
instinct pushes to its peculiar satisfaction as any
other instinct does. On it is based obedience. It
is the existence of this instinct extraordinarily
developed by drill, that has given to Germans their
amazing subordination to their ruling class, and their
remarkable readiness to accept their opinions as
well as their modes of behavior from above. Part
of this docility is doubtless through training of fear,
but only indirectly through using fear to stimulate
into action the instinct of self-subjection itself.

Many parents develop this instinct in their children with slight appeal to fear. Obedience becomes phenomenal where this instinct is developed directly, and without recourse to fear. Some men can be held to obedience only through the direct action of fear, they seeming to be defective on the side of this instinct of self-subjection, while others possess it in such unusual strength that they are easily controlled and learn to obey without fear. Those possessed of the instinct of self-assertion in great strength, and being also weak in the instinct of self-subjection, cannot easily be trained into obedience. If they be strong also in pugnacity, not even fear, indeed least of all fear, can reduce them to order. They are by inborn nature made inevitably rebels against all control, and are likely to be hung in civil life, or shot in the army, and it is best so.

But there is another form of this instinct of self-subjection which I have named "follow the leader." It is the basis of what has been called hero-worship. We see it at work in the boy gang, where the leader is followed and his will obeyed with pleasure and often without ever any exercise of the instinct of fear, and without any consciously exercised self-assertion of the leader, or self-subjection on the part of the members of the gang. Some of each there may be, but in some happily gathered gangs neither appears to any great degree. Authority is exercised on the one hand, and obedience rendered on the other without friction and with a spontaneity and pleasure in it that is extraordinary. This may be an extreme and unusual case. Let it be granted. It serves, however, to make clear the point in hand.

Now given this instinct operating in its two forms, it can readily be seen how effective will be those three general tendencies that seem to grow out of gregariousness. The suggestions of the leader, the contagions of his emotion, the imitations of his acts, will work with great effectiveness. His commands, his enthusiasms, his behaviors will be found in the members of his gang, as a matter of course. Fear of him will scarcely be in evidence The less, the better. The more readily will a common set of ideas, common feelings, a common form of actions be found among those who follow him.

Now let us transfer this to the training of an army. The point to be held firmly in mind is just what is to be trained. It is not the instinct of fear which is to be made the basis of discipline of the best sort. It is the instinct of self-subjection in its two forms, of submissiveness, and following the leader, both of which are in most men, though not in all, agreeable in exercise and also in the satisfaction of them. The rank and file of the best army is to be trained by appeal to these instincts and not to fear except in a certain degree. Of course, certain men (they are few in numbers) can, as has been remarked, be controlled by fear alone, and one might think that they had better be shot than kept in the army. Other places of action may perhaps be found for them.

Having, then, the army as a crowd, the task is to train it into group action, action as a group and for such action as is for the benefit of the group. This requires obedience, on one side submissiveness of all to orders for such action as is for the benefit of the group, and on the other side, in its very best form, enthusiasm in following the leader in those actions. Such training, based on intelligence and lofty sentiment in the rank and file and, above all, on enthusiastic following of the hero-commander, will make soldiers who will be ready to die for their cause, but they will not be likely to suffer panic.

There may be added here the operation in connection with these instincts, that of self-assertion, and also of the sentiment of self-regard in the many forms in which it may appear in soldiers so trained. These forms may be listed as follows: (1) the sentiment of the sacred cause, (2) regard for himself as the embodiment of that cause, (3) then again for himself as a man in whom the honor of his regiment and army is at stake, (4) still further for himself as a man to whom certain manly behaviors are a matter of course. So the training due a soldier, especially in a free country, goes beyond that drill which brings about group action, the very core of which is obedience. It means training in sentiments, into those structures of mind, often, too often, neglected, through the scant intelligence of officers and their total ignorance of the complex structure, and manner of organization, and ways of behavior of the minds of their men.

Attention should be called to the psychological significance of some of the things done in military affairs, inherited from the past, and done perhaps without altogether understanding why. Officers may be helped to discover perhaps that, in using these practices ignorantly or abusively, they defeat in a measure that very end for which, through the experience of long ages, these practices have been found to be useful means.

Take first the matter of distinctive uniform of officers and the various insignia of their ascending rank. Psychologically in enforcing obedience through using suggestion, prestige of the man who gives orders is important. His dress, his badge of ranking office makes that order to be not his, but that of the army. This is particularly true in the army of a democratic nation. The commander-in-chief is but the representative of the army as a whole, even more he stands for the whole people whose army that is. The voice heard in an order is not his own. It is the army's, it is the people's. It is the same down to the drill sergeant. Thus distinctive uniform and insignia strengthen prestige, increase suggestibility in men and officers to those marked as above by bar or star, hat band or epaulet. The same is true of insignia of distinctive service, of heroic deed. The instincts of self-subjection, not only of submission, but much more so of follow the leader work effectively, and preparation of mind to receive orders comes into existence, and alacrity in response follows.

The strict enforcement of the rule of salute is of the same psychic nature. It fortifies the activity of the same instincts of self-subjection. It habituates the men and lower officers in their degree to the mental attitude of readiness to obey. That it is never to be omitted, always to be done, is in order that the attitude of preparedness to receive orders may be ever at hand. It is using the law of exercise which controls habit formation. As this habit is peculiarly artificial and arbitrary, it is easily lost, so exceptions are not allowed.

To the bystander looking on, the harsh voice in which orders of the drillmaster are given, his seemingly too-frequent and loud-voiced scolding for petty offenses or apparently none, his overindulgence in profanity at the men's expense — all this seems strange and absurd. It is a tradition with officers of very ancient date. The psychology of it may be that the instinct of self-subjection in its inferior form is so set working and fixed in a firm habit of readiness to receive orders and carry them forward into action swiftly and easily. I have said the instinct "in its lower form." This suggests that the ancient tradition is not very intelligent. It has come down to us from armies made out of slaves of despots, or subjects of sovereigns, not out of citizens of a free, self-governing state. Russian and German armies are still trained by the officers exciting through fear the instinct of self-subjection. The code of training of Frederick the Great was made up of "the most brutal and degrading punishments." And to a large extent in Germany these still obtain. They are, happily, largely gone from the American code. The men of various races and nations who went from East Side, New York, to Camp Upton, with the terror of army discipline before their eyes, as that discipline was known to be in their native lands, I am told, came home on furlough enthusiastic for army life. They had been well fed, their health cared for, and they had been treated with strange consideration by their officers. They felt themselves made actual comrades in arms with their officers, and not subjects to arbitrary and petty orders given by ill-natured superiors, who, in a free country, are held to be no better than themselves.

This suggests that the development of the instinct of subjection, in its higher form of follow the leader, is of more value in the training of the soldier than its lower form of submission. It suggests also the stupidity of the drillmaster of whatever rank, who makes his appeal only to this lower form, who thinks by inspiring fear, by punishment, by rough treatment and annoying manners and acts, he can win obedience. Too often it is the assertion of his authority ill-naturedly to the satisfaction of his own Prussian love of power, without the humanity that belongs to the citizen-officer of a free country. Some roughness, some degree of inspiring of fear and enforcement of harsh discipline may be necessary to all, and much of it to a few, but it may be doubted if the ancient traditions that still hold in the armies of even free peoples, traditions that have

come from the Frederick the Greats of the past, is
not only an anachronism, but renders the best
results of military training impossible. The saying
of Wordsworth that "We live by admiration, hope
and love," is not without an immense value, because
true even in the life of the soldier, whether in the
ranks or the lower grades of command, since he
there and then also may best live in love and admiration of his officer

Another instinct there is, as has been suggested
above in passing, which can be made to play a great
part in the effective training of the soldier and his
officer. It is that of companionship. To make his
men his comrades, without losing standing as their
commander, is the quality that is found in the most
valuable officer. It is that, as said before, that has
made the New York City East-Sider, foreign born
or foreign hearted, not only a proud, brave and
capable American soldier, but has tended also to
make his parents, his brothers, and neighbors
American citizens. And in this connection should
be recalled to mind the powerful part that the
development of comradeship among the soldiers in
the ranks plays in courage of heart and hand. To
the establishment of this among soldiers careful
attention should be given. Men with such relations
hearten each other, help each other more in attitude
of spirit than in helping hand. Napoleon once
remarked of his soldiers that they had not eaten
together often enough.

This suggests the whole matter of choice and

special training of officers. For at last in the con-
fusion of battle oftener than not it is the officer
who turns the tide. It is his manifest courage that
becomes the basis of the courage of the men. Here,
again, those three general tendencies of suggestion,
contagion of emotion (sympathy) and imitation
have great effectiveness. The officer's coolness, self-
command, evident intelligence control the situation.
This is particularly true of the officers of the lower
grades, for in battle, when the line is broken up
into squads, and the officer can be heard and seen
only by a few, it is captain, lieutenant, even sergeant
or corporal who counts. Fortunate is that army,
that people, whose general level of development in
intelligence and character is high. The material
from which are drawn officers and privates is of the
best. The soldier has solid basis for confidence in
his officer, as the officer in his private. And the
officer is aware, as his training should have made
him, that above all things he is to his men the model.
This means that, in the highly excited and sensitive
condition into which his men are thrown in danger
which evokes fierce instinctive fear, he is to be the
suggester to his men of ideas of action, the infector
of them with emotion, the doer of acts that are sure
to be well nigh mechanically imitated by them. It
is he that must not fail the soldiers of his group, his
army, his country. He surely is afraid as are his
men, but he exhibits mastery of his fear.

There are many examples illustrating the psychological effects of this action of officers. "Grant,

when his men who were constructing intrench-
ments under fire and were fast getting out of hand,
coolly walked to the top of the intrenchment and
sat down in plain sight to smoke a cigar. That,
without a word, was sufficient to steady his men."
At Pickett's charge at Gettysburg, General Gibbon
rode down the lines, cool and calm, and in unimpas-
sioned voice said to his men: "' Do not hurry, men,
and fire too fast; let them come up close before you
fire, and then aim low and steadily.' The coolness of
their general was reflected in the faces of his men.[10]"
But in the turmoil the higher officer's act is soon lost
to sight. It is then that the under officer's action is
big with destiny. He holds the outcome in his own
resolute will and inspiring example. There and then
he seems to be the most important man.

CHAPTER XII

The Restoring of Courage When Lost

It was shown at the close of Chapter V how exposed is man to the utter breaking down of his courage, because of the ancient origin and great strength of his instinct of fear. Many men are born with this instinct in relatively abnormal strength, and so seem fated to life-long exhibitions of cowardice. It is no more their fault than it is a fault to be born with dull eyes, or short legs. All men, quite without exception, are born with this instinct strong to an uncomfortable degree. The man in whom it is weak is unusual. The man born without it, if one ever was, would be a monstrosity. Thus all men in certain conditions, quite without exception, are liable to sudden, perhaps for a time utter, loss of courage. This must be accepted as a fact of our natures, and provision is to be made for its occurrence, and methods of recovery are to be sought for and when discovered used. To a large extent both the discovery and the use of such methods are in man's power, "For man is man and master of his fate."

Now first it may be observed the law of habit works here as inevitably as elsewhere. It is well known that horses acquire the habit of running away. It is fear and its flight fixed as a permanent structure. It is found that when fixed it is well-nigh useless to try to cure it in a horse. But in man, owing to the capacity he has for building sentiments in the technical sense, it is possible to give the so-called born coward control of his fear mechanism. The coward schoolmate mentioned in the first chapter becomes a fearless dispatch bearer through storms of battle. A sentiment of regard for himself, as a man of that quality, arose in him, and there was nothing else to be done by him but what a *man* should do. So also was it with the ambulance driver, turned "yellow," reported in the same chapter. His friend awoke the submerged sentiment of his manhood, showing him that it was instinct that carried him away, as it may any man of a sudden in strange, confusing situations. The Croix de Guerre was his then as though fated to him.

The method is then meeting instinct by sentiment, even when the instinct of fear is fixed into habituated cowardice. With change of social environment, where one is not known to be any other than a man, one may take a new start, and once showing himself what it is taken for granted he is, the way is clear for courage and heroism. The confidence of one's friends in a man, their intelligent appreciation of what misfortune befell him, is to him salvation. It is comradeship here that first helps one to be brave, and after weakness restores his strength. The care-

ful building of sentiments of honor, of loyalty to
one's professional calling, to one's friends, family,
country, and above all of self-respect, *i.e.*, regard for
one's self as a man who is a man, forestalls cowardice, and if perchance it of a sudden overwhelms one,
furnishes the source of restoration. And the way
to win this for one's self is through the companionships a man selects and to some extent through the
careful self-discipline to which he subjects himself.
For others than one's self, the method is much the
same, appeal to sentiments already in them, rebuilding them when broken, or creating them where they
do not exist.

The endeavor to restore courage in battle or even
elsewhere by overcoming one fear by another greater
fear, to meet troops fleeing from probable death in
front by threat of certain death in the rear, may
be, as a temporary expedient in an extraordinary
situation of panic, of some advantage. But to make
it a settled policy is to confess that the army has no
courage except in the lowest of all forms, the instinctive fear of the physical consequences of being afraid.
When a commander has to order the shooting of his
own men to keep them fighting, the end is near.
Punishment, which is appeal to fear, is only good as
a temporary expedient. Courage to live, and to live
well, comes not from jails, scaffolds or hells. It
comes from sentiments of regard for the approval
of good and brave men, and most of all from regard
of a man for himself, as one who cannot run from
duty, nor from any difficulty, enemy, or suffering.

It often happens that in battle, owing to strange, sudden and confusing situations, fierce terrors overwhelm a man. In such a case, the sentiments on which his life has been securely based are not at hand. He acts at the instant from ancient inborn instinct. We are wont admirably to express his condition by saying he was beside himself, or not himself, as though the man he really is was not at the time present. In fact, that is precisely the case. The *man* proper is his system of sentiments. Outside of that he is kin to the beasts of the field, and as acting then and there he is as the rabbit scurrying in terror to cover. Now it may happen, and it often does happen, that an emotional disturbance when very intense, breaks down, for a time more or less long, the sentiments on which a man's life is wont to be based. At least if not broken down, they seem to be submerged into what we call the unconscious part of a man's structure. As they were lost in battle, they seem to continue lost thereafter. How long a man is likely to remain in this condition, or whether he may ever recover from it depends in part upon the original and acquired fibre of the man, and in part also upon the violence and length of continuance of the terror shocks to which he has been subject.

There are two forms of this undoing which may be studied separately. The first is that which appears in many soldiers who, after their experience in war, take a slump, lose self-respect, enterprise, ambition, spirit. They tend to become dependents, parasites on society. The courage that is gone out of them is not so much that which overcomes fear, as that which faces difficulties. They supinely settle down to indifference and to be taken care of. Sometimes this attitude grows into claiming support as their right, as though having done a national service, discharged a public duty of great difficulty and through great danger, they were thereafter released as a matter of course from any further service, had no longer any duty to perform. There will surely be found thousands of these men in all countries after this war. Some of them are already appearing even in America, so recently entered into the great contest. The problem will be before all nations, what is to be done with them? The answer is in most cases that it is a problem of re-education, of rebuilding sentiments of self-respect, of patriotic service, of public obligation, of manliness. This, of course, is no easy matter with grown men. And all the more so as the public attitude toward returned soldiers is quite certainly to be one of softness. We shall quite likely mollycoddle all manliness out of many of them. It will, therefore, be a first pre-requisite of their salvation to educate the public, i e., to build in citizens at large a strong sentiment of regard for manliness as belonging pre-eminently to the soldier-hero home from the wars. It belongs to him no less but rather more than to the home-stayer far from battle perils and hardships.

The community and the government are quite awake as to their obligation to the soldiers crippled

in battle or otherwise seriously incapacitated for
normal life. These will be trained to skill in self-
support and so to service, to duty, and saved from
loss of self-respect, being made able, that is courageous, to face life's new and greater difficulties. But
for those not crippled in body, but who through
violent emotional experiences, particularly of terrors, are strangely changed in mental structure, the
case is not so easy. To all outward appearance
whole of body and also sound of mind, so far as
ordinary intellectual activities are concerned, they
are victims of perhaps an even worse wounding than
the maimed in body. They have suffered serious
impairment of higher structures of mind. The
nobler sentiments are gone, or are weakened. And
these must be replaced or strengthened. This is no
easy matter where schools of training may be impossible, or where attendance on them is not likely
to be enforced, even if they could or would be established. It will be necessary to fall back on the
discipline of that school of life in which all are
trained, and in our social attitude, and by preaching in newspaper, magazine and book — not only
in the at present far too ineffective pulpit — to
exact a requirement which all, even our returned
soldiers, must fulfil Beyond this, in laws and
penalties against the idler, a policy already adopted
in certain states against loafers and tramps, whether
they be rich or poor, there is an instrument effective
against moral ruin. This seems particularly cruel
when applied against our soldier boys, and so there

is little likelihood that it will be applied, though so
necessary to the moral well-being of these heroes
and to the social health of the community in the
days that are to come.

Something should here be said on the general
effect of a pension system for the soldier who has
done special and perilous service for his country.
It is natural that gratitude and generosity, especially when bestowed out of the public purse, should
be ungrudgingly offered to our heroes home from
the war. But there has ever been a danger to the
beneficiary in its effect on him from the point of
view of his character both as a man and a citizen.
Too easily he slides into a dependent, feeling his
country owes him a living, forgetful that even after
his great service he still is in service and obligated
to do his part toward giving others a living, provid-
ing not only meat for their bodies, but high example
for their souls. One's duty for today and tomorrow
is not discharged because he did his whole duty of
yesterday. That one was heroic in the trying conditions of war does not release him from the call to
heroism, self-respect, and honor in the common-
places of everyday life. Even those maimed in
battle, while receiving proper compensation from
the State for their immense sacrifices, should still
be asked to bear themselves with some of the same
hardihood and courage in the continued and to
them not easy difficulties of daily life. A system of
pensions, as well as a public attitude toward them
that allures them unconsciously into supineness of

will and uncourageousness of heart toward life's requirements is rather a moral curse to them than a benefit.

The other form of loss of courage which it was proposed to discuss comes from the violent emotions of fear and horror due to the extraordinary conditions of recent warfare. This form of it has been named "shell shock," though it arises not only from the violence of high explosives, but may be found appearing under extreme strains in other conditions, and in certain cases even before terror of actual battle has been experienced. The cases thus named have been grouped in several classes, only one of which concerns this treatise. The others are clearly not psychological but physical. It might be well to describe briefly some of these physical cases in order to make clear the character of that class which is to be considered here.

There are cases in which the violent explosions, as examination shows, destroy the nerve structures of the brain and so cause death. In other cases the atmospheric pressure, removed suddenly after the instant of explosion, sets free gases in the blood, which as bubbles plug the finer arteries feeding the brain. In still others the explosion acts like a blow on the head, for the time arresting consciousness or impairing its normal action. Others there are which show the effect of gassing from the carbon monoxide released by the high explosive. All these classes of cases, it will readily be seen, are mechanical in their causes. Whatever psychological after-effects occur

arise from physical causes. Their treatment is, of
course, directed primarily to physical restoration,
after which, if further treatment is needed, it will
be the same as in the class now to be studied.

There are the many cases in which the derangement is primarily mental, and in which the cause of
derangement is certainly in large part extreme,
overwhelming terror and the horror of ghastly
sights. Some of these cases are not caused by high
explosives, though many of them do appear in such
circumstances. The name of "shell shock" for
these cases is not, therefore, rightly applied. They
appear sometimes in training camps, where shell
shock is impossible. They are found in men who
give way to long strain of apprehension, who, of
highly sensitive organization and vivid imagination,
do not need the terrors of actual battle or the sudden violent explosion of a large shell to throw them
into this condition. Causes purely personal and
non-military, when added to the intense emotional
disturbances of war, may bring about this condition.
For example, men who have done well, to all appearances, in meeting the conditions of warfare, may be
thrown into this state by news that their wives have
gone away with other men. Add to all this that in
civil life like cases occur in certain conditions, and
it at once becomes clear how unsuitable for them is
this name, shell shock.

But however that may be, the fact that the cause
is plainly in these cases rather psychological than
physical, and that the effect in very many, if not

all, of them is loss of courage, brings them into consideration in this treatise. We are first to get some clear idea of what has happened. Courage, as has been shown repeatedly in this work, in all cases above the instinctive level, arises from the control of sentiment over the instinct of fear however set into action. What has presumably happened in these cases is that the accumulation of effects of long-continued terror and horror, motor expression of which has been suppressed, or the violent rush of them in sudden shock, breaks down in some way these structures of sentiment which are the basis, the very essence of control. It is universally recognized that violent emotion tends as we say "to unsettle the mind." That means that the structures of sentiment on which action has been based theretofore may be impaired or changed in that way. Men, after such an experience, often become different. Religious conversion, which is really change of mind-structure, comes often in that way. A great or violent love passion may make one man into a hero, another into a criminal. So a great emotional terror, even if it does not make a once brave man a coward, may at least take courage out of him, not only as ability to face perils, but also as nerve to overcome difficulties, and as fortitude to bear adversity.

Granting that this is what has happened, that sentiments which overcome fear have given way under prolonged strain or sudden shock, the remedy becomes clear. It is to rebuild these impaired

structures. Unfortunately there are some cases
where the derangement is so complete as to render
all recovery impossible. The methods by which
this can be done, in cases where it is possible, can
only be discovered by experiment. But it is much
to know just what has to be done. And these methods
are to some extent already known, and it is found
that they vary from case to case depending upon the
temperament and personal life history of each man.
The author of this treatise is not competent to
undertake any detailed enumeration and description
of these methods, some of which are now discovered,
many of which are still in process of determination.
Only a few indications of what is being done can be
here attempted.

It is recognized that "immediately after the onset
of the attack, the patient passes through a very
critical period." His condition is naturally such
as to degrade him in others' and his own eyes. It
might be surmised that punishment and ridicule
would aggravate his case and render his cure less
likely, and this for fact is found to be the case.
The danger is that, according to the law of habit, a
structure of his mind begun under the emotional
stress may become fixed, and other related structures
may grow up with it and the case develop into a
chronic incurable disorder. Too much emphasis cannot be laid upon the evil of ridicule and punishment.
Good soldiers are thus lost, sometimes shot, often
made into confirmed cowards, and what is worse,
they who might be good citizens in profession, trade,

family life, are sacrificed to vulgar ignorance of companions, or unintelligent treatment of officers and surgeons, and made incompetents for life or moral malingerers.

To prevent fixation of the state produced by the shock, immediate treatment, and in the near vicinity of the battlefront, is found to be successful in most cases. "Recovery within the sound of artillery or at least 'Somewhere in France' is more prompt and durable than that which takes place in England." (Salmon.)[11] Sending them back to the general hospitals in the rear, where the stay is apt to be long, has proved a mistake: the longer the sojourn, the less likely is the recovery. The conditions there make for invalidism, because there is not to be found in these institutions the skill to understand and the skill to educate, i.e., to rebuild these injured sentiments. This requires, as has been shown by Dr. Salmon, much special expert training and detailed attention. He writes: "Efforts must first be made to gain an understanding of the personality — the fabric of the individual in whom the neurosis has developed. His resources and limitations in mental adaptation will determine in large measure the specific line of management. The military situation is most striking, but the problem which life in general presents to the individual and the type of adaptation which he has found serviceable in other emergencies, are of as much importance as the specific causes of failure. The disorder must be looked at as a whole. The particular incident . . .

whether shell explosion, burial or disciplinary crisis, must receive close attention, but not to the exclusion of other factors less dramatic but often more potent in the production of the neurosis. . . . The medical officer's attitude is of much importance. He must be immune to surprise or chagrin. Although understanding sympathy is nearly as useful as misdirected sympathy is harmful, he must always remain in control. . . . The patient must be reeducated in will, thought, feeling and function. Persuasion, a powerful resource, may be employed directly, backed by knowledge on the part of the patient as well as the physician of the mechanism of the particular disorder present." This is a clear recognition and forcible statement of the fact that certain disorders are primarily psychological and that their treatment — which may be called mental medicine — is re-education, which is rebuilding certain impaired mental mechanisms.

In this undertaking re-education by physical means is valuable, but the end for which such occupations are employed must be kept ever in mind, whatever they be for bed, indoor or outdoor patients. They must never be made substitutes for full activity of all functions of the normal man. As soon as possible, productive should be substituted for nonproductive work. Such activity of thought and hand as will develop and strengthen the sentiments that are to overcome the emotional terror should be sought out for each case. The sentiments most important for the soldier are those of regard for himself as a manly man, a patriot — a man of self-respect and one worthy of the respect and honor of his fellow men and particularly of his soldier comrades.   He should be admitted into conscious partnership in this high undertaking, and urged and encouraged to do his own, which is the greater part, in rebuilding such sentiments. For a time, perhaps, no suggestion may be made of his return to the fearful situation in which his stroke came, but not for long should such a forecast be allowed him, lest the shrinking from the ordeal become a fixed habit and the man become incurable.

This suggests the danger in too great manifestations of sympathy and pity. However commendable in the kindly disposed nurse, relative or comrade, these are likely rather to hinder than to help toward restoration. Just what degree of hardness and apparent lack of sympathy is required can be determined only by the trained skill of the wise nurse, physician and friend to whose lot falls this re-education and cure.

The danger which is to be avoided in the treatment of this particular type of loss of courage is that of creating in the soldiers at large an impression that there is in this manner a way of escape from the terrors and horrors against which only with extreme effort can they stand up.

The knowledge that thousands of their comrades have been discharged from the army because of this reason may not unnaturally work toward weakening the power of resistance of men, who are desperately holding on and seemingly to the last grain of their strength. Not so much consciously would they give way, as by subtle unconscious working of suggestion would they find themselves in collapse. It is the opinion of Dr. Salmon that these cases would be enormously increased by a treatment that failed to return most of them restored to manhood and courage, to the firing line. But outside of cases so weakened would be the effect on men of unheroic mold who would consciously undertake in this way to seek escape. Such malingerers are for the most part easily detected by the trained expert. But small opportunity should be given them to play this attempted rôle. Every such would be malingerer held steadfastly in the ranks, every self-deceived hysteric undeceived as to the nature of this breakdown of his courage, and restored to conscious and willing courage, and every truly broken man rebuilt into manhood and returned to the firing line to take his place as a good and brave soldier, fortifies just so much his hard-pressed comrades, reduces by his presence the likelihood of the collapse of others, and hastens the day when the terrors and horrors of this war, and may it be of every war, shall come to an end. Upheld by the solid structure of such a sentiment, there will be courage to carry this thing through and past the agony to the new world of peace we catch glimpses of beyond.

CHAPTER XIII

EPILOGUE — MORALE

SOMETHING has been said in passing, here and there, in previous chapters, about Morale. The very name itself implies that it is in reality a matter of character, of morals. It is an exceedingly complex condition, which can be understood best as a fundamental form of sentiment, in the technical sense employed in this book.

Let us repeat briefly again, to make sure that we understand, what is meant by a sentiment. It is not simply an idea, a thought in the intellect, though that is involved. Ideas by themselves do nothing, effect nothing. Nor is it an ideal of conduct which by itself arouses emotions but not action. As Goethe remarks, "With the mountains in our eyes we love to walk along the plain." We love to repeat the lofty ideals of conduct in the Lord's Prayer, it makes us so satisfied with ourselves. But we may never lift our hands masterfully, if at all, to make God's "will be done on earth as it is in heaven." We are apt to take it out in emotional excitement, mostly mild. This using ideals for agreeable emotional experiences is what we call sentimentalism. Not till we have a structure of

145

mind involving at once and together ideas for intellect, emotions for heart, and action for hand, do we have sentiment in the technical sense. It is a mechanism that ideals set acting into emotions and deeds. Now morale is a comprehensive sentiment in that sense, a structure for certain thoughts that arouse certain feelings, and quicken to certain deeds, to broad ideals in feeling and act rather than merely to rules that govern details of social life. It is a matter of major morality, of loyalty.

But also it is not generally understood that morales differ. They are built out of different ideals awaking different complexes of emotion, and different deeds. Some morales are better than others. They are better because more permanent, less likely to disintegration and destruction, as well as better because the deeds that characterize them are of higher social value. This has been made clear in Chapter VIII, where the courage of differing patriotisms was discussed. But in Chapter XI it was shown that, beside the kind of sentiment, for an army elements of intelligent skill in one's job are necessary. But not only for armies and warfare is this necessary, but in life generally for individual and State, sentiment must add to itself intelligence and skill. If the individual is not to suffer disaster, fall into panic, lose his head, do the fool thing, he must be practically wise and skilful. It is the same in matters of government. In revolutionary epochs, for example, lofty and generous ideals of justice, of "liberty, equality, and fraternity" may be plentiful, even sentiment in the technical sense may to a certain extent be present. For example, it was in the French Constituent Assembly on the great night of August 4, 1789, when nobles, the aristocracy of state and church, in intense emotional fervor, gave up their privileges to become equal citizens in the equal liberties of equal brotherhood. But alas! there was neither the well-knit fibre of sentiment, nor the trained political skill to carry into active performance an aspiration so lofty in conception, so nobly felt. There followed in due time panic, as there would in an untrained army, no matter what its ideals and sentiments. There came the "Reign of Terror," in which those who attempted to rule were in even greater fear than those whom they ruled and made afraid. It is the same today in Bolsheviki Russia. The ideals, we may presume, are in the main high, but the intelligence in public affairs is lacking, the trained skill of those who would administer affairs does not exist. In panic terror they find dangers on every side. They may have abolished capital punishment in deference to kindly human feeling, but they wildly attempt to save themselves and their misunderstood cause by murder and massacre.

There was in revolutionary France for a time no national morale, as there is none in Russia today. There were ideas, even ideals, but no well-built sentiment to respond to these, no trained skill to realize them in practice. Morale as now understood is a matter of slow and painful upbuilding. National morale may require centuries to construct the minds and train the skill of its citizens. England with its

> "Freedom slowly broadening down
> From precedent to precedent,"

has for nearly a thousand years been ever building a national sentiment, a national mind, which has been at once the living constitution of her government, and the morale at the bottom of her civil and military order. She has passed through revolutions without reigns of terror. She has had her fears, but they have not degenerated into panics. She has stood firm and unshaken through long and severe strains, and has saved the free civilization of Europe more than once from destruction. Her morale has been at once characterized by growing ideals of justice, and developing practical skill in public affairs. And remarkably today are exhibited her characteristic steadiness against assault, her growing intelligent, practical skill.

So also the France of 1914-1918, without panic, with immense endurance and extraordinary skill of civil statesman, military commander, and common citizen and soldier, has faced appalling odds, and for courage and intelligence has astonished the world, and made herself loved and admired of all right-minded men. The morale of her army rests securely on a firm foundation of the prior and broader national morale of her people.

But it was said morales differ. The morale of Germany is not that of England or of France.

Wonderful structure that it is, so patiently and diligently and in its way skilfully built up by conscious effort in school, university, and army, it is lacking in certain elements of humanity, which to England and France have been of priceless value. These inborn elements of kindness, which lead to justice and mercy, are not really lacking in Germans, though for the time suppressed. They inevitably in the long run will assert themselves even in Germans, and in asserting themselves will tend to disintegrate the structure of mind from which they have been left out. Hindenburg asserted at the beginning of the great war, that in the last analysis the outcome would be a matter of nerves. In physical structure, no people seems better made than the German soldier, nor any soldier in the world was ever more carefully and intelligently trained in his profession. But his action was to be based on the sentiment of power for power's sake, and by methods of frightfulness that would strike terror into the enemy, and bring swift disintegration of his morale.

We do see disintegration setting in as Hindenburg affirmed it would, but not in the Allies, whose morale is built of more numerous inborn human elements, and with the more humane elements dominating, and whose morale has been strengthened by the very methods by which it was thought it could be undermined. No frightfulness on the war fronts, no propaganda in the rear can do other than strengthen the morale of nations whose cause is the cause of humanity, of justice, of brotherhood.

Already U-boat commanders release their captives, instructing them to inform Americans that they are "not baby killers." Learned professors who, under the whip of imperial authority signed lies, begin to exhibit shame and misgiving. Voices in the press are being raised against policies and methods once approved and gloried in. Certain statesmen are beginning to look with suspicious favor upon President Wilson's statement of what must be the outcome for justice to oppressed peoples of Germany's great war inaugurated in lust of material power. A morale that can be sustained only by a government-inspired press, by falsehood and deceit, has at bottom a fundamental weakness. Doubt must be inevitably bred by the very methods that are used to support it. At the heart of national policy must be felt to be the people's welfare and an unimpeachable sincerity. A shaken faith in that policy, in that sincerity is a supreme national peril. And when doubt comes, morale crumbles. Then courage alike of citizen and soldier weakens and at last fails utterly.

If a comparison should be made between the United States of the Civil War and of the present World War, the change in morale would be found extraordinary. Great and unyielding as it seemed then, the depth, strength and pervasiveness of it as revealed today amazes even those who had most faith in the virtues of their country. Both on the sides of sentiment and of trained skill a vast change has taken place. A partial catalogue of differences will expose something of the heart of the nation.

Today, enlistment is for the duration of the war, not for a term. That to which they have set their hand they will perform, no matter how long be the tremendous task.

The nation without resistance has accepted the draft as the manner most just and effective for every citizen to acknowledge his country's will to protect and establish the sacred principles of democracy. There is no buying substitutes, and little shirking of personal duty. And this draft has been administered everywhere by local civil voluntary boards in recognized fairness.

Men of ability and large affairs that bring them great incomes give up their offices and emoluments to offer their services, often with no pay, or with little, to the government, and for as long as that service is needed.

Taxes most extraordinarily heavy on the rich are accepted without murmur, and Liberty Bonds at low rates of interest are bought in amounts so vast as to run beyond imagination.

Bankers, who formerly exacted from the government hard terms for selling its bonds, render now the heavy service freely and without emolument.

The industries of the nation are regulated and used by the Government for the enforcement of the nation's will, in a way beyond the imagination of even those few who have dreamed of such an order of things as possible only in some remote future. All that has been asked is that regulation be just.

And for our men in battle there is national insurance, the best equipment, the highest pay, from the State. And from organizations outside of Government, the Young Men's and Young Women's Christian Associations, the Knights of Columbus and the Red Cross have undertaken with wise skill, great enthusiasm and at immense outlay the task in every way possible to hold up the courage, comfort in distress, supply needs no government can minister to, so maintaining the morale of the soldier while expressing the morale of the united people.

This catalogue has not been made in the interest of glorifying America, but as exhibiting evidences of a developed strong morale not suspected, and surprising even to the people who, though they had it, were unaware of its strength. Men of America who recall the Civil War exclaim: "I do not recognize my country!" This condition of affairs so unsuspected is only possible through the existence of a strong sentiment that is other and more than that of patriotism. It is a sentiment of justice, ideal, emotional and skilled in practice — a sentiment democratic and therefore international, of an order for the world guaranteeing security for America, for her peace, prosperity and spiritual welfare, and not only for America, but for her allies, and even her enemies.

President Wilson, in his address in New York on the night of September 28, has given in words the clearest, most forcible expression of this American morale, as the nation during the past year and a half in practical administration has embodied it in a vast army and navy overseas; and as that army and navy have demonstrated it in redoubtable courage and executive efficiency on the field of battle and at sea. It is for the future to demonstrate the reality of this sentiment, the enduring quality of our morale. It is the nature of a morale of this structure to be indestructible in defeat, and rise even from a grave in which temporary disaster may seem to bury it.

NOTES

1. Prof. E. L. Thorndike, in his *Educational Psychology*, has shown that in the earlier years of a child no such equipment appears as McDougall claims. The activities then are far simpler, and less coordinated. It may be granted. But in the same way it can be urged that in the early weeks of the child's life in the womb no such bodily equipment is found as belongs to the new-born babe. Does that prove that the baby's limbs, viscera, brain are not its original equipment? All turns on the meaning of the term original equipment.

2. Modifications in McDougall's list have been made. They are three: (1) His instinct of self-subjection has been recognized to include two forms of which he does not seem to be aware. (2) The instinct of companionship as distinct from gregariousness has been added. (3) So also I have added the instinct of rationality.

3. Prof. W. S. Woodworth in his admirable little book, *Dynamic Psychology*, as against McDougall, has given good grounds for including the push of rationality as belonging to the original equipment of the human mind.

4. Quoted from Major Eltinge's *Psychology of War*, p. 105.

5. Mr. A. F. Shand, in an article on "Character and the Emotions," in *Mind*, N. S., Vol. V, first formulated this theory of sentiments on which

McDougall based his *Social Psychology*. It is the only satisfactory treatise on that subject so far known to the author.

6. Ribot, *Psychology of the Emotions*, p. 19.

7. Quoted in *The Evolution of Prussia*, by Marriott and Robertson, p. 228.

8. See Appendix.

9. Quoted from Dr. Grudden's *Crowd Suggestion*, in Eltinge's *Psychology of War*, p. 31.

10. Eltinge, p. 101.

11. Beside the quotations in the text, many suggestions of value have been taken from Dr. Thomas W. Salmon's "The Care and Treatment of Mental Disease and War Neuroses in the British Army," in *Mental Hygiene*, Vol. I, No. 4.

APPENDIX

A School-Made War

GERMANY has revealed to the world the appalling power of a systematic thorough education in building a patriotism of a certain sort. A sketch of that education ought to be enlightening to such as are not familiar with it. It will suggest an explanation of Germany's part in bringing on and manner of conducting the World War. But, more than that, it ought to suggest the intelligent use of systematic education in building a patriotism whose root is justice and not power.

The outline of German education which follows in part, written by James L. McConaughy, President of Knox College, appeared in *The Boston Transcript*. To both acknowledgment is made

To enslave the German people into intellectual, as well as physical, submission, the military aristocracy has made all schools state institutions, has made all teachers state officials, powerless to think or act for themselves, and has even made the actual subjects in the schools help to carry out this aim.

Decades before any other nation did so, Prussia put all of her schools under absolute government control, thus preventing the establishment of any independent schools which might teach freedom of thought or action. Since the government wishes all future citizens while they are school pupils to think alike and to think as the government dictates, private schools are in effect forbidden; no private school in Germany can be opened without government approval, and this is very seldom given. Bismarck, who built the foundation of the Germany of today, maintained that the government's greatest

hold upon the people could be secured through the
schools, for "he who controls the schools, controls
the future." The present Kaiser thinks likewise;
his interference with the courses in the gymnasium
was caused, as he frankly stated, not for educational reasons, but because he believed the classics
did little to develop German patriotism: gymnasium
and *Volksschule* alike were to be under the absolute
dictatorship of the government. So effective have
the schools proved in extending the government's
domination over the people, that the same scheme
has been tried for countries outside of Germany. A
society was started in 1886 to advance German
education in other parts of the world. Before the
war it had sixteen hundred centers for the teaching
of German, German patriotism, and German learning. One of the most fertile fields was the United
States. This society, although it naturally kept its
activities under cover, is responsible, says Collier, for
the introduction of German into five thousand American schools, enrolling six hundred thousand pupils.

*   *   *   *   *   *

To control the schools, and through them the
pupils of the nation, Germany early saw to it that
she had complete hold upon the teachers. Accordingly, the German teacher was made a civil servant.
When he secures his position he is forced to take an
oath which forbids him to do, write or say anything
subversive to the interests of king and state. No
matter what his individual opinions may be, he is
bound, body and mind. This is even more true of
the university professors. They are in effect government slaves. The government has the power
of removing or reassigning them. In such a strat-
ified economic order as Germany's a man who is
expelled from his position in middle life can hardly

hope to even make a living in any other way. There
is, therefore, nothing surprising in the subservient
spirit demonstrated by the world-known university
professors who, early in the war, signed the docu-
ment exonerating Germany from all blame, even
although later events have shown that they were
not given the evidence of Germany's innocence
which they desired; they knew that their livelihood,
and possibly even their lives, depended upon doing
what the government directed.

In addition to absolutely dominating the schools,
the government directs that school instruction be
made to serve its ends, by the definite teaching of
patriotism, by the inculcation of "love" for the
Kaiser, by the disparagement of other countries,
by the glorification of all things German, and, even,
recently, by teaching the Pan-German ideal. Quotations from German school manuals (given in
Scott's *Patriots in the Making*) clearly indicate the
position of patriotism in the curriculum. In the
normal schools future teachers are trained "to learn
to understand and love the Fatherland, its ordered
life and institutions, that they may become qualified
to arouse and to nourish in their pupils love
for the Fatherland and for the ruling dynasty."
In geography "the greatest stress is to be laid on
the knowledge of the Fatherland, its character, its
political divisions, its civilization, and its commercial relations." Patriotism, in other words, is
officially made a part of the curriculum. In the
readers there is constant glorification of the German
"heroes" of earlier days. The child has scarcely
learned to read before he is deluged with stories of
the wars and victories of his country. Poems are
memorized extolling patriotic deeds. One of the
most popular justifies a man who killed another
for uttering criticism of the Fatherland. One-

third of the material provided for the first class in
the gymnasium is patriotic   The two great school
holidays are the emperor's birthday and Sedan
Day.   The walls of the schoolrooms are covered
with pictures of the emperor, the empress, Bismarck and battle scenes, among the most popular
of which are prints of German soldiers bringing in
wounded French prisoners in the War of 1870.   The
singing of "Deutschland über Alles" is resorted to
many times each day.

* * * * * *

Naturally, the best subject through which patriotism can be infused is history.   The aim of the
teaching of history in Germany is exclusively to
increase the pupils' knowledge of the glories of the
Fatherland.   Accordingly, for such an aim there
is no impropriety in definitely distorting history.
The German historian, Prutz, frankly says that
much of the history taught in the German schools is
"in conflict with the highest law of history, with
truth."   He criticises the panegyric way of teaching
history, which makes all of Germany's rulers
"equally great as diplomats, administrators and
soldiers."   Frederick William, in 1799, in describing
the proper methods of teaching in the *Volksschule*,
said regarding history: "It should limit itself
solely to the most important national events and
have no other purposes than to awaken patriotic
love and affection, pride in the deeds of our fore-
fathers, and the desire to emulate them."   In the
elementary school, history is designed to plant "in
the minds of the children the sense of German citizenship, love of country, allegiance to and admiration of the ruling house."   Naturally, efforts must
be made to awaken on the part of the elementary
school pupils an enthusiasm for things military,
because the boys of this school must provide the

empire with its soldiers, and the girls must become
the mothers of future German battalions. The
history teacher makes that class the liveliest of the
day; patriotic selections are often recited; the
teacher, says Alexander, frequently becomes so
enthused by his subject that he would seem to us
more like a Fourth of July orator than a school
teacher. The Franco-Prussian War provides material for much of the history course; so much have
the Germans glorified this war that even we Americans often forget that a few years before it took
place we had a war in America where in one battle
more men were killed and wounded than in all the
battles Prussia has fought from 1860 to 1914. Prussia's prowess in this war is more a result of distorted
teaching than actual fact.

* * * * * *

Obviously there is nothing in the German history
course to promote any knowledge of or desire for
individual freedom. Frederick William IV said
in 1849, regarding the revolution of the preceding
year, that the teachers were responsible for it. Germany's rulers, accordingly, took pains to see that
such a condition should not happen again. In
1890 the Kaiser announced at the famous educational conference in Berlin: "The school ought,
first of all, to have opened the duel against democracy." This incident, quoted by Van Dyke, proves
the extent to which any possible teaching of liberty
is excluded from the German schools; the German
school authorities desired to introduce as a school-
book a life of Goethe written by an American,
Boyesen; they stipulated, however, that the chapter
in it discussing Goethe's love of liberty should be
eliminated; when the truth-loving American scholar
refused, the authorities forbade its use in the German schools.

A very large amount of the German teaching of patriotism is personal, aimed to instill loyalty to the emperor and to the monarchical principle upon which his power is based. Elementary school children are taught poems of love for the Kaiser, with such statements as these: "The Kaiser has many soldiers; he loves us all; we love him, too." "Here and beyond we were, we remain thine, Lord and Emperor." All of the references to the Hohenzollerns make them out as absolute heroes who can do no wrong. Their house is said, in one of the schoolbooks, to be the greatest foundation of the German empire. Another teaches that only grateful devotion to the empire can maintain the State upon the heights she has attained. In the lower schools of Prussia the regulations require the use of a text-book that will show "how the monarchical form of the State is best adapted to protect the family, freedom, justice and the welfare of the individual." School children are taught that one of the worst crimes that can be committed is *Majestäts Beleidigung*, criticism of their ruler.

The schools also aim to glorify all things German. There is never a suggestion that the Germans have ever been defeated in warfare. It is also implicitly taught that, in every war which Germany has waged, she has been defending herself from the aggression of her enemies, and that the shield of the Fatherland is spotless. The history of other nations "is to be considered only as it is of importance for German history." Instruction in the German schools ignores all points of view except the German. A German school geography contains the statement that "the Germans are the civilized people of Europe and that all real civilization elsewhere is due to German blood."

* * * * * *

The Pan-Germanic dream, even, has entered the German schoolroom. Schoolboys were taught that the German empire of today should include all the territory in Charlemagne's kingdom. A school geography states that Switzerland, Belgium, Holland, Netherlands and Luxemburg are really inhabited by Germans, although now detached from the old German empire to which they once belonged, and to which they must be returned. Throughout all the teaching, the implication is that the Germany of today is only a small part of the real German empire. To extend the Pan-Germanic idea, colonies are necessary, and Germany is described in the schoolbooks as a great colonizing nation. One geography states that Germans are the historic colonizers; that Germans conquered Venezuela, which should be part of Germany today; that a German designed the first maps of America and gave the land its name. The most popular geography, hundreds of thousands of copies of which are used, says, "Universal history shows that the prosperity—yea, even the existence—of States is dependent only upon colonization."

It may finally be noted that German school practices, as well as German school subjects, go far toward proving that German education caused the war. The discipline in the German schools aims only at obedience; the teachers browbeat the pupils and punish them. When pupils so trained become soldiers and are freed from restraint, the atrocities at which the world has been so shocked naturally result. The German schoolboy gets no training in appreciation of or reverence for woman. It is rarely that he has a woman teacher. The religious instruction in the school is a mere sham and hypocrisy. There is no expectation that the character of the pupil will be influenced; the secondary school teacher's congress, not long before the war, passed a resolution to the effect that the school had nothing to do with the formation of character.

The German schoolboy gets no training in fair play. He has no sports. Those that have been attempted have resulted in such hatred between contending schools that they were abandoned by official edict. A German schoolboy's word of honor amounts to nothing. The masters are spies and there is no expectation that the students will do right unless compelled to. Spying, indeed, is one of the great characteristics of the German school; it is expected that boys will "tattle-tale" on one another; the son of an attache of the American embassy in Berlin was expelled from a German gymnasium because he refused to tell tales on his fellow pupils. The masters spy on one another. The schoolboy is one of a group, never an individual. He never asks questions of his teacher. "Listen to me, so that you can tell me back what I am telling you," shouts the German teacher to his pupil. The government thinks for him and regulates his every action. During the week the school teacher is in charge of him, even during the recess period. On Sunday the state-controlled minister instructs him.

Education, instead of enlightening the German nation, has debased and dehumanized it.